Do Not Be Afraid

Do Not Be Afraid

The Healing of Fear

MICHAEL BUCKLEY

Blessings
Michael J Buckley

DARTON · LONGMAN + TODD

First published in 1995 by
Darton, Longman and Todd Ltd
1 Spencer Court
140–142 Wandsworth High Street
London SW18 4JJ

ISBN 0–232–52111–5

A catalogue record for this book is available
from the British Library

Acknowledgements
Biblical quotations are from *The Jerusalem Bible*,
published and copyright 1966, 1967 and 1968, and *The New
Jerusalem Bible*, published and copyright 1985, both by
Darton, Longman and Todd Ltd and Doubleday & Co. Inc.,
and used by permission.

Phototypeset in $10^1/_2/12^1/_4$ pt Baskerville by Intype, London
Printed and bound in Great Britain by
BPC Wheatons Ltd, Exeter

We ourselves have known and put our faith in
God's love towards ourselves.
God is love
and anyone who lives in love lives in God,
and God lives in him.
Love will come to its perfection in us
when we can face the day of Judgement without fear;
because even in this world
we have become as he is.
In love there can be no fear,
but fear is driven out by perfect love:
because to fear is to expect punishment,
and anyone who is afraid is still imperfect in love.

1 John 4:16–18

Contents

Preface

Fear is the enemy of freedom. It is the destroyer of personal happiness and personal identity. It prevents us from becoming our own person because it hinders us from discovering who we really are. It hides our potential from us. After a long and painful search I think I have come to terms with fear in my own life. I know what it has done to me over the years. I hope that at long last I have escaped from its clutches.

For years, perhaps without being aware of it, I passed on my fears to my congregation. I never thought of setting them free because I was not free myself. Fear had made me a prisoner within myself, and in turn the warder of others to whom I ministered. I was high on law and religion but low on love and faith until healing entered my life and changed it. I know now in the deepest part of my being that to be a Christian you have to be free to be yourself as God means you to be. If we are not free then we are not human. Today I am 'my own man'. I want to share that liberating experience with as many people as possible, and it was for this purpose that ten years ago I founded the El Shaddai Christian Movement for Inner Healing.

Why have we called it El Shaddai? It is the most ancient name given to God by the Jews long before he spoke to Moses on the Mountain of Horeb. Its exact meaning is not certain, but for the Patriarchs it meant that God was

'Almighty' and that nothing was impossible to him. It also means 'The One of the Mountain' because of the ancient Jewish belief that God lived on the mountains in high inaccessible places, enshrouded in cloud and mist. I see the healed person as an eagle who has learned to fly in freedom and fulfilment in the high places where God lives. The parent eagle teaches its young how to fly, so God our Father teaches us what true freedom is and the power within ourselves to find it.

Many people today are crippled within themselves because they have never experienced the freedom of being themselves which comes from the awareness of God's love and purpose for them. They are eaglets afraid to stretch out their wings and fly because this not only means their leaving the security of their nests, but also the danger of falling. Freedom involves risk of the unknown and makes people stay where they are, and so they never achieve the purpose for which they were born. Like the frightened eaglets, there are many people today who are filled with irrational fear which triggers off in them an overpowering sense of guilt, unnecessary tension, despondency, depression, hurtful memories, insecurity and a thousand and one other things which bring their lives to a standstill and prevent them from being human. They are prisoners. In the El Shaddai Movement we encourage them to break the bonds that fetter and limit their lives. From experience they know they cannot do it alone, and so we share with them in a loving, encouraging, caring, gentle way until they discover for themselves how free they can become once they realise that God is their Father who wants them happy and free.

Through our missions and services of healing we help people to be aware of the possibilities of positive change in their lives. They are encouraged to foster a new vision of themselves, of life, and of their world. They discover a belief not only in God but in themselves. Books and tapes have grown out of El Shaddai experience and in them people have found a chord of response which relates to their own lives and fears. They too experience a healing force in their lives.

Everything that is written in this book is based on the experiences of those who have shared with us in the El Shaddai Movement. Without them, this book, indeed our Movement, would not be possible.

I am grateful to Morag Reeve, who over the years cajoled and badgered me to write down my experiences of inner healing; to Margarette Chilcott and Rosemary Wainwright who gave generously of their time to type it, and to Oonagh Watters who shared with me in all our El Shaddai healing missions throughout England. Ultimately the inspiration came from El Shaddai, The God of the Mountain, who heals us as without fear we fly where eagles dare.

Fear of Healing

There is a deep-rooted fear of healing. I have sympathy, not condemnation, for people who are trapped in this form of fear. Basically they are ignorant of what healing really means, and what it does to, or for, the person. It is not their fault. They have been victims of false teaching and prejudice. Healing is an unknown quantity for them. What you don't know about gives you cause for suspicion. You begin to believe stories of weird happenings in healing so that all people in the ministry of healing are tarred with the same brush. Healing is looked on as a form of 'white magic' which is best left alone.

It is difficult to cope with this negative, strongly held attitude. People won't listen because as a rule, especially in matters of religion, they are slow to accept change. Their minds are set firm as concrete. They think not only that healing is not right for them, but that it is just not 'right'. It is not God's work. They have never experienced healing in their own lives so why should they believe that it happens to others. They cling to what they have and healing does not figure in their notion of God. If they had a favourite hymn it would probably be 'O Thou (not you) who changest not abide with me'. They distrust any signs of adventure or challenge in the practice of their religion. They have got on without healing up to now so it is best to leave well alone. They are afraid of venturing beyond the familiar. They are 'traditionalists' in the wrong sense of the word. Religion is a duty handed down by their parents, and as a rule they would avoid all forms of joy and adventure. Religion is a private and very serious affair, mainly of avoiding sin, and all forms of emotionalism are to be avoided. Religious services are not happy occasions. You go to worship God because it is your duty. Healing is for Pentecostalists and megastar American evangelists who claim all sorts of miraculous happenings. People fall down all over the place with noise which would do credit to witch doctors and their followers (victims). If that is what is meant by 'healing' they want no part of it. Neither do we, but when we use the word 'healing' this is what people have in their minds and it is our duty to spell out for them quite clearly what we mean in El Shaddai by inner healing.

How then do we explain healing to people who do not believe in God, or, if they do, have so neglected its ministry in their own churches that they treat even the word 'healing' with suspicion? The best thing is to find another way round the psychological barrier and use different words to explain what healing really is. So we start by saying that *healing concerns itself with the quality of life*. No one should disagree with that. We should all want to live life as fully as possible. What is important is not the number of years we live, but the way in which we live them. From the moment we are born until we die we have a right and an obligation to live as perfect a quality of life as possible in the current circumstances. *'The glory of God is man fully human, fully alive'* is a sentiment often expressed by Christians. God does not want us just for the next world; he wants us for this world as well. That is why he sent his Son to live on earth. God so loved the world that Jesus became man to improve our quality of life. He looked after people's earthly as well as spiritual needs. His first miracle was to turn water into wine: he improved the quality of the wedding. More than once he fed people miraculously in the desert. The coming of Jesus on earth gave a quality to human life which God intended we should have. We are not angels; we are human persons. Healing, therefore, concerns itself with every aspect of human life, it deals with the body as well as the soul. It does not ignore the natural circumstances in which we live and helps us in every way so that nothing, whether it be poverty, violence or some other disruptive force, can destroy our quality of life and make us less of a person. Jesus was perfectly human and he wants us also to be fully human, fully alive. Christian healing cannot ignore any aspect of our lives which is related to how we live in *this* world. Too often we have concentrated so much on the spiritual side of our lives that we have ignored our day-to-day living in this world. We deny the full force of Jesus becoming man if we see it only as a call to live in the next world and not an example of how we were meant to live in this world.

What can we do as Christians to improve our quality of life?
First, we must *love ourselves*, and see our lives as having meaning and purpose. If we don't love ourselves then we cannot love anyone else. It is true that we will never be completely whole, totally healthy, in this world, but we can come to terms with those things in life which would otherwise hinder our growth as persons. We rise above them and learn to live with them. We may never be 'cured' of our false guilt, irrational fears, our physical or emotional disease or the hostile environment in which we are forced to live out our lives, but we will still remain persons with a distinctive quality of life. The Bible is full of stories of people who overcame the most horrific handicaps and *became* great persons. We know from our healing services that the human spirit will not be quenched, and we have seen people grow through suffering and become more fully human.

Secondly, we need people to love and be loved by them. They are necessary for our quality of life just as we are for theirs. The community or family is where we share our lives together in all aspects. We are our brother's keeper and we need to see that he is treated justly because we love him. Jesus, when he saw the crowds hungry in the desert, said to Peter, 'It is for you to give them to eat'. We have tended to forget that we are all brothers and sisters in the human family who share one world. Our quality of life depends on each other. There is no neutrality. We cannot step aside when we see the wounded traveller on the road to Jericho. We have to stop and help and be prepared to give more if and when it is required. It is in giving that we receive a deeper quality to our life.

Thirdly, we know, even more in recent times, that we live in a violent hostile world. Peace is necessary for the quality of life and the world is antagonistic to it both within ourselves and in others. Jesus suffered at the hands of hostile people. If God did not spare his own Son then he will not spare us. We cannot live our lives in a stockade protected from the outside world. The example of Jesus' coming on earth and facing his enemies with courage and gentleness is the only way to be at peace within ourselves. We live in a 'war situation' but the weapons we use are love, compassion, sensitivity, hope, encouragement and all those healing elements which make people aware that there is a quality of life which they too yearn for deep down in their hearts.

Fourthly, for us as Christians our quality of life, our healing, comes from God our loving Father. It is difficult to talk about him to those who don't believe. As a rule, when we want to help someone find himself it is best to start with a natural human factor. A doctor friend of mine helps people more by the compassionate way he treats them rather than by any medication. His patients tell me, 'It is the way he looks at you that you know he understands your pain and wants above everything else to make you well.' In healing we should never rush in immediately with the spiritual answer. We start where people are and move on from there. We try to help them where they hurt.

What do we mean by 'healing'?

Once we have spoken about healing in the general terms of improving the quality of life it is necessary for us as Christians to probe deeper because healing is of the essence of the Christian gospel. In our sick world of violence and depersonalisation there are few who think of healing. For the majority of people the world has always been as 'bad' as it is today. To talk of the healing power of God who really cares for us and wants us to be healed, healthy, is to fly in the face of reality and history. It is, they say, the escape mechanism Christians use in order to avoid acknowledging the inevitability of useless suffering in human life which in itself has little hope of purpose or fulfilment. For them there is no God and therefore no healing and in the final analysis no quality of life except that which you can secure for yourself, albeit at the expense of others. It is a case of the survival of the most selfish and greedy while the poor and humble go to the wall. A world without healing is a world stripped of Christ's message as if he had never lived among us.

This fatalism is infectious and has deeply affected the mentality of many Christians who, having abandoned the practice of Christian healing for centuries, are today strongly opposed to its increasing acceptance and practice among many of their brethren. These Christians, without being aware of it, are in fact turning their backs not only on the gospel of Jesus, in which healing is essentially enshrined, but on the practice and belief of the Church for many centuries after the end of the apostolic era. In historical terms, distrust of healing in the churches is a relatively recent phenomenon.

Historically, in order to understand Christian healing, we need to go back to the origin of man. It is essential for our concept of healing to believe that as human beings we are unique in our world and are special because 'God created man in the image of himself' (Genesis 1:27). God had a purpose for the human race and the world which he had made. He wanted his first human persons to be healthy and he blessed them, saying, 'Be fruitful and multiply, fill the earth and conquer it. Be masters of the fish of the sea, the birds of heaven and all living animals on the earth ... God saw all that he had made and indeed it was very good.' (Genesis 1:28, 31) The true purpose of creation was, and is, wholeness, health. We as persons were meant to be healthy, to be at ease with God our Father, with our neighbour and within ourselves. But we are obviously diseased, not at peace with life within or outside ourselves. So what went wrong with God's plan?

The answer is, quite simply, *sin*. God created us free. *Freedom* was God's unique gift to the human person. To take away our freedom is to destroy us as persons. Man's sin was his refusal to obey God his Father: 'Sin entered the world through one man, and through sin death, and thus death has spread through the whole human race because everyone has sinned' (Romans 5:12). The human family tree became diseased in the Garden of Eden. Man frustrated creation to such an extent 'that it was made unable to attain its purpose' (Romans 8:20), and though wounded 'it still retains the hope of being freed, from its slavery to decadence, to enjoy the same freedom and glory as the children of God' (Romans 8:21).

Our hope of health is centred on God's promise of healing through the Messiah who will restore and heal our broken relationship with:

- God, whom we will acknowledge and trust as our loving Father;
- our neighbour, whom we will love in a new restored friendship;
- ourselves, in our *soul* by forgiving our sins; our *emotions* by mending hurtful memories, stress, tension,

irrational guilt and uncontrolled fear, all of which cripple us as persons once we let them control our lives; our *body* by curing illnesses which prevent us from living full human, healthy lives, or bringing them under control so that they do not diminish us as persons.

Since we are diseased as persons in all aspects, we are also healed as persons in the same way. Because healing involves the whole person then the spiritual, emotional and physical healings of the person are all interactive. Fear, for example, when it gets out of control affects not only our emotions, but also our bodies and our spiritual lives. Fear-filled people do not really love in human terms as Christ would have us do because his type of love casts out fear and set us free to be more fully human and alive. A healthy person is one who is living a higher quality of life than he would if he were still diseased. Christ, by his life, death and resurrection, gave a new dimension to the word 'healthy'. The ultimate aim of all Christian healing is to heal the person in his totality, which ultimately includes giving thanks and glory to God the Father who, in his mercy, through Jesus Christ restores us. Through healing we become more fully Christian. In this sense, as we understand healing at El Shaddai, no Christian should reject healing if he wishes to remain true to the gospel. He may oppose the manner in which the actual healing ministry is exercised, but not the concept of Christian healing itself, which is necessary for our Christian lives. It is our oxygen which we breathe to stay alive. We are aliens in a world which is hostile to us and our way of life restored by Jesus Christ. We are the victims of the disorder caused by sin, and the prisoners whom Jesus came to set free by his life, death and resurrection.

For many traditional churches the only form of 'healing' which they will accept is spiritual 'healing' such as is received in the sacraments. Physical 'healing' or curing,

...happens, is regarded by them as exceptional and ...e fostered only in special places of pilgrimage, or ...vidence of unique holiness in extraordinary people. But even these people are to be regarded with suspicion during their lives in case they develop a cult following, or eventually turn out to be less than genuine. It is the cautious approach which discourages physical and emotional 'healing'. This approach seems all the more necessary in recent times with the upsurge of new Pentecostal churches. These latter churches emphasise physical 'healing' to such an extent that it becomes the criterion of their authenticity as the true Church of Jesus Christ. Their motto is 'no miracles, no Christ, no Church'. Healing, therefore, has become an area of contention and division between the churches because we have not defined clearly what we mean by Christian healing. There is no point in rejecting or accepting healing unless you know what healing really means. We all need healing if Christ's Church, and world, is to become united and fulfilled, and if we are to be truly free, human and Christian. A priority, therefore, is to be healed of our fear of healing.

The word 'healing', as I said, is very much misunderstood because basically we do not understand the true nature of sin and how it affects our lives in a hostile world. It was so in Our Lord's time and life. It is the same today. People in the Christian Church and outside it often equate healing with physical or emotional cures. Yet there is a world of difference between 'healing' and 'curing'. *Curing concerns* itself with *one aspect of a person's life. Healing deals with the whole person* in its complexity. Curing is undoubtedly a help to a person's healing and can lead to it. Jesus cured the ten lepers, *but only one of them was healed* because he realised the source of his curing. He showed he was healed by returning to give thanks and glory to God. Doctors, for example, concentrate on curing the body, psychiatrists the mind, priests the soul, social workers the circumstances or environment in which a person lives. *Only God can heal the person,* because only he who created man can recreate, restore, renew and make him whole again as a person. Curing, as it were, removes the obstacles to healing. The psychiatrist by his skills can, for example, remove the emotional blockages and so *prepare* the person for healing.

We believe, as Christians, that there is more to a person than just a body or emotions. Each person is unique as a person and has an extra personal dimension to his life which God alone can change. Then what about healing? Have we no part to play in this as Christians? God gives the *gift of ministry, or preparing,* to his people so that, together with Jesus Christ, they can share in helping the person to become whole. We must never claim any more power than that for ourselves. Ministers help, God heals. No one is a healer in his own right or by his own power.

Christ came into our wounded world so that *every aspect* of our lives would be healed. Without this healing we would not be able to live life to the full. For Christ, healing a person's body is as important as healing a person's soul if the body hinders the person from living the full human Christian life of inner peace. It is the person who is healed of his hindrance, whether the healing be of body, emotions, spirit or soul. In the famous case of the paralytic Jesus first cured his soul then his body (Matthew 9:2–7). But this does not mean that there is a priority in healing. Body and soul are equally important in healing because they are both parts of the human person. The soul does not take precedence over the body, or vice versa. Jesus healed the paralytic as a person, so he cured his body as well as his soul.

Fullness of life does not necessarily mean that we are always cured completely in our minds and bodies. The ultimate aim of all healing is to make us aware of God the Father's abiding love for us. Despite all the healing we receive, we may still be physically handicapped emotionally distressed or live in a spiritual desert, but healing makes us aware that even when we walk in the valley of darkness, Jesus, the Son of the Father, is with us because he has been there before us. *We are healed as persons.* In healing we share in Christ's triumph over death because his loving Father raised him high as our victorious healing Lord. We rise above our disabilities whatever they may be and live a full, human, Christian life.

Let me give you an example of someone who, though still physically damaged, is enjoying true fullness of life which he received through Christian healing.

Jim was a well-known and highly respected footballer. His attitude to his sport was one of complete dedication and soon he was the idol of the young people who saw in him the kind of sportsman they wanted to be one day. Unfortunately he was seriously injured by a very danger-ous tackle which meant that he would never play football again. His whole attitude to life changed so completely that he became a different person. He made life miserable for his wife and children. He was so bitter because of his accident that he turned his back on the game he loved so passionately before. Full of self-pity he was destroying himself with depression, and alcohol. Eventually his wife persuaded him to come to an El Shaddai healing service and by God's grace his whole approach to life was restored and renewed. He went back to the football ter-races to support the game that for so many years had been so much a part of his life. The influence he has today on young people is as great as he ever had on the football field. He certainly experiences fullness of life. He is healed as a person even though he is not cured of his physical disability. The fact that he is unable to play the game he loves so much no longer prevents him from living his life as a full, human, Christian person. He knows that he is a better person today and living a fuller life than he did when he was a nationally acclaimed soccer star whose physical fitness was essential to that role. His body is healed in so far as it does not interfere with his life as a person; he has been able through God's power to integrate it into his life.

Why wasn't Jim cured as well as healed? If God really loved him why didn't he work a miracle and enable him to play football again? It has been done for others, so why not for him? I don't know why he was not cured, but his life as a *person* is changed. He has got his relationships right within himself, with his family and with God. What happened to him is part of the consequence we pay for living in a hostile world which does not want our wholeness and inner peace. We are all damaged and need to be healed, but why can this only be achieved by God? The simple answer is that he created us and when we became damaged by sin, only he could recreate us. In God's plan the true purpose of creation was, and is, wholeness. Everything in the beginning came from God and was ordered and healthy. Man was the perfection of creation because he was uniquely chosen to praise and love God as his Father. So that he could do this, God created man free. To be human, man had to remain free. This gave him the wonderful opportunity of freedom of choice, a gift that no other living creature possessed, and in this freedom, he came closest to God himself. While all other creatures obeyed their instincts, man alone could choose, by the use of his intellect and will, to do what he wanted. So while the rest of creation obeyed, man through sin disobeyed. He said to his Creator, 'I will not obey you' and through his disobedience the priest of creation turned upside down the world God left him. So our human nature became diseased, and inordinate fear entered into the depths of our personality. Freedom and fear were in conflict. Like many other things in our disordered, diseased life, fear went out of our control. It controlled us rather than our controlling it. The world does not want us to be free and uses fear to control and diminish us as persons. Healing puts it into its proper perspective so that we can use it creatively and positively.

Sin, which in its essence is man deciding to become the sole master of his own destiny, destroyed the true relationship of love between the person and God, set brother against brother in the human family and destroyed the wholeness of man as a person, leaving him at war within himself. It is towards recovering this true relationship with God and ourselves that all Christian healing is directed. Later in this book we will deal with the havoc caused by destructive fear in these relationships. Christ healed us and our wounded world of everything, including fear, that would prevent us from being whole, human, Christian people. Healing is necessary so that we can live the full life of inner peace. *As in creation, now we have to choose to be healed because God wants us to have freedom of choice* in our lives, in a world in which the effects of sin would keep us prisoners. It is a freedom won for us by Christ and we have to learn how to claim it and use it. That is our main function as Christians who have experienced healing and wish to help others, especially those who are near and dear to us. We are always being asked in the El Shaddai missions as to precisely what we are doing in healing. We are simply encouraging and helping people to believe that God is their Father who loves them and wants to heal them. We help people to believe in and love themselves, no matter how physically or emotionally handicapped they may be. They come to terms not only with themselves, but through forgiveness with their neighbour also. Forgiveness is an essential quality we all need if we want to be whole persons. The person at odds with his neighbour because of culture, religion, politics, colour or a thousand other divisive factors, is a fragmented person. Healing takes us beyond the boundaries of denomination so that we see the gospel of Christ as uniting and unifying his healing force for all his people who call him Lord, and acknowledge God as Father. The gospel is alive today for those who really want to continue Christ's work of helping his people to grow as persons in their own right. Healing is an end to superstition, 'faith healers' and those who neither understand the gospel nor comprehend the beauty and awesome dignity of a human person. In the Father's eyes all his children are beautiful and he wants them to be whole and fulfilled in their lives, not only in the next world, but in this one as well. It is for this purpose that the risen Christ in his power and presence is with us always, healing and restoring his wounded brothers and sisters who come to us seeking healing in his name.

2

Jesus and Healing

Jesus was a healer. This was how he was known and remembered. The word 'healer' epitomised his life's work. All that he was in himself and his life-style brought a healing influence to all those with whom he came in contact. Healing was not an extra in his life, something he did in addition to his teaching in order to support his message. It *was* the message. Jesus was not a politician; his manifesto about his mission of freedom, which he proclaimed in the synagogue at Nazareth at the beginning of his public life, was not just words or empty promises. It was the work he came to accomplish.

> The spirit of the Lord has been given to me
> for he has anointed me.
> He has sent me to bring the good news to the poor,
> to proclaim liberty to captives
> and to the blind new sight,
> to set the downtrodden free,
> to proclaim the Lord's year of favour.
>
> (Luke 4:18–19)

He fulfilled all his promises beyond people's wildest dreams. They hungered for what he had to offer and he fed them through his healing. His message about liberating people was actually achieved through his healing power. He did not talk about healing. He actually healed. Because actions always speak louder than words, his

FOR GENERAL PRACTITIONER'S NOTES

CONFIDENTIAL

Ms. Agnes P Cooper
8 Johnstone Pk, Inverkeithing, Fife, KY11 1BT

Rosyth Health Centre
Park Road, Rosyth, Fife, KY11 2SE
Tel: 01383 418931

If you cannot collect your Prescription
yourself please give WRITTEN AUTHORITY

to the person collecting on your behalf

There are 3 items on this re-order form 23/04/1999

1. THYROXINE tabs 50mcg
TAKE ONE DAILYFOR ONE WEEK THEN 2 DAILY
You last asked for this on 23/04/1999. You may ask for this
item 1 more time(s) without being seen..

---

2. CLIMAVAL tabs 1mg
AS DIRECTED
You last asked for this on 23/04/1999. You may ask for this
item 1 more time(s) without being seen..

---

3. PAROXETINE tabs 20mg
1 DAILY , 28 DAY DISPENSING
You last asked for this on 23/04/1999. THIS REPEAT PRESCRIPTION
HAS EXPIRED. It must be REAUTHORISED before any further
prescriptions..

End of re-order form for 3 items

AS FROM 11.01.99 PRESCRIPTIONS WILL ONLY BE ACCEPTED BY
TELEPHONING 419007
MONDAY - FRIDAY BETWEEN 11 - 12 & 3 - 4.30.

actions were his words: 'What I say to you I do not speak of my own accord: it is the Father, living in me, who is *doing his works*' (John 14:10) and 'If I am not doing my Father's *work*, there is no need to believe me; but if I am doing it, then even if you refuse to believe in me, at least believe in the *work* I do; then you will know for certain that the Father is in me and I am in the Father.' (John 10:37–38)

Healing wounded people like us was his Father's business and Jesus made it his lifetime's work. 'That evening, after sunset, they brought to him all who were sick and those who were possessed by devils. The whole town came crowding round the door, and he cured many who were suffering from diseases of one kind or another; he also cast out many devils, but he would not allow them to speak, because they knew who he was. In the morning, long before dawn, he got up and left the house, and went off to a lonely place and prayed there. Simon and his companions set out in search of him, and when they found him they said, "Everybody is looking for you".' (Mark 1:32–37) From that morning in the synagogue at Nazareth until his death on the cross, when he forgave those who crucified him, his life was totally dedicated to healing. If you take the healing out of his gospel there is no message, no life, left.

Everything about Jesus had a healing power, to the extent that even his clothes became instruments of healing. 'Now there was a woman who had suffered from a haemorrhage for twelve years; after long and painful treatment under various doctors, she had spent all she had without being any the better for it, in fact, she was getting worse. She had heard about Jesus, and she came up behind him through the crowd and touched his cloak. "If I can touch even his clothes," she had told herself, "I shall be well again." And the source of the bleeding dried up instantly' (Mark 5:25–29). He healed people in such a powerful way that it was obvious to those around him who were not blinded by bigotry or jealousy that here was no passing holy man or prophet. ' "Here is a teaching that is new," they said, "and with authority behind it: he gives orders even to unclean spirits and they obey him." ' (Mark 1:27) 'They were all astounded and praised God, saying, "We have never seen anything like this".' (Mark 2:12) The miracles of Jesus' healing created the impact needed to convey to people the immense power of his Father's love at work in him. It was unadulterated love for people. Healing was the expression of his love for the people and for his Father. He loved those he healed and it showed. 'A leper now came up and bowed low in front of him. "Sir," he said, "if you want to, you can cure me." Jesus stretched out his hand, touched him and said, "Of course I want to! Be cured!" And his leprosy was cured at once.' (Matthew 8:2–3) Jesus knew that his Father wanted the leper to be made whole, healed. Also, because Jesus was a man himself, he was sorry for him. It was this dual love and compassion of Father and Son for the sick person which cured and healed him. Jesus always healed people for their own sake. He knew what they meant as persons to his Father who had created them and whose will it was that they should be recreated, renewed, through healing. Jesus wanted people to be whole and healthy so that they could lead the new life as freed children of their Father whom he loved. Their healing gave his life meaning and purpose.

When we say that Jesus healed, what exactly do we mean? To understand, we need to look at Jesus as a Jew in the background and culture of his time. He healed persons as persons. The Hebrews, among whom he minis-tered in his public life, did not think of a person as divided into body and soul, but as a whole person with body, soul, feelings and a personal historical background stretching back in the human family tree. For them, to heal a person was to heal them as a whole person. Chris-tian healing, in the same way, involves a person's whole world. It is a restoring of *soul* by forgiving us our sins and helping us to let that forgiveness flow out to others. It relieves our *emotions* by setting the person free from hurtful memories, stress, irrational guilt and all the other emotional upsets which disturb our peace as a person. The *body* is also cured of physical disease or defects which hinder people from living a full human life.

Nothing in the make-up of the human person was excluded from Jesus' healing power. He healed whatever in them prevented them from living whole human lives. He was not a soul or a body healer. There was no priority in his scale of healing. Both soul and body were equally important to him. The classic example is that of the healing of the paralytic.

> Some people appeared, bringing him a paralytic stretched out on a bed. Seeing their faith, Jesus said to the paralytic, 'Take comfort, my child, your sins are forgiven.' And now some scribes said to themselves, 'This man is being blasphemous.' Knowing what was in their minds, Jesus said, 'Why do you have such wicked thoughts in your hearts? Now, which of these is easier: to say, "Your sins are forgiven", or to say, "Get up and walk"? . . . he said to the paralytic – 'get up, and pick up your bed and go off home.' And the man got up and went home. A feeling of awe came over the crowd when they saw this, and they praised God for having given such authority to human beings. (Matthew 9:2–8)

Jesus discerned that the man needed to be cured of his paralysis as well as forgiven for his sins in order to be healed as a person. Those who separate, dichotomise, the soul from the body, or see one form of 'healing' as more important than another, do not understand what healing meant to Jesus. Such a division, or order of priority, is totally alien to the gospel. Jesus looked on the person to be healed *as a person*. Here he saw the man's paralysis as being as great an obstacle to his wholeness as his sins were. He loved the person lying before him on a stretcher; he knew his needs and met them at both levels. This is the *full* gospel which he bequeathed to his followers. They were to do what they had seen him do (John 13:15). They were not to settle for anything less. In fact Jesus promised that 'whoever believes in me will perform the same works as I do myself, *and perform even greater works*' (John 14:12). No one was excluded from his healing power except those who excluded themselves through minds and hearts closed by prejudice, bigotry, cynicism or disbelief in his power and willingness to help them. Jesus went to his home town of Nazareth. 'He began teaching in the synagogue and most of them were astonished when they heard him . . . And they would not accept him. And Jesus said to them "A prophet is only despised in his own country, among his own relations and in his own house"; and he could work no miracle there, though he cured a few sick people by laying his hands on them. He was amazed at their lack of faith.' (Mark 6:1–6) Jesus placed no limits on his healing power. It was his listeners who frustrated his ministry and denied him the right to heal in his Father's name. Jesus believed that nothing was impossible for God, his Father. He loved the people he met more than anyone else could, but he would not force them to believe in him or to trust him.

The secret source of Jesus' healing was his unfailing love for people no matter who or what they were. He did not come just for his own. No one was outside the scope of his healing love, whether they were Jew or Gentile, Samaritan or Syro-Phoenician. He was more than willing to meet their need as soon as they acknowledged it. Healing was for him love in action. It was the outreach of his Father's love for him and for the people he met: 'As the Father has loved me, so I have loved you' (John 15:9). He wanted to do his Father's will and he knew that this was to make people whole through love. He was one with his Father, so there was no obstacle to impede the outpouring through him of his Father's love for people. He was a perfectly clear conduit. For Jesus there was no healing without love of the wounded person who came to him for his ministry. His followers were to use the healing ministry as an expression of their love not only for the sick, but also for each other: 'By this love you have for one another, everyone will know that you are my disciples.' (John 13:35) Healing of others in love will dry up when and if his followers do not overflow with love for each other. Healing is as simple and as demanding as that. It is love that heals because it changes everything.

Whenever Jesus was approached in *faith* by anyone for healing for themselves or for others, he never refused them because they believed in his power to do what they asked of him. 'Two blind men followed him shouting, "Take pity on us, Son of David." And when Jesus reached the house the blind men came up with him and he said to them, "Do you believe I can do this?" They said, "Sir, we do." Then he touched their eyes saying, "*Your faith deserves it*, so let this be done for you." And their sight returned.' (Matthew 9:27–30) The centurion who wanted healing for his dying servant sent messengers to Jesus to plead his cause. He said he was not worthy enough to have Jesus enter his home, but as a man himself subject to authority, he acknowledged his belief in the power of Jesus to heal his servant. 'When Jesus heard these words he was astonished at him and, turning round, said to the crowd following him, "I tell you, not even in Israel have I found faith like this." And when the messengers got back to the house they found the servant in perfect health.' (Luke 7:9–10) Jesus saw all his healing as an expression of his belief in his Father's willingness to answer his prayer of faith for those who came to him for help. He was completely confident that whatever he asked would be granted. There was no 'hedging of bets' when Jesus prayed for healing. He stepped out in faith time and again to heal in his public life and never once did his Father let him down.

He encouraged people, especially his disciples, to have *faith* in God. This was the key factor in his life and healing. Jesus was without question a man of faith. Time and again his faith was set against his disciples' fear. On one occasion they were out in a boat, when a storm broke out over the lake so suddenly and violently that the waves were breaking right over the boat and the disciples feared they would drown. Jesus was asleep. 'So they went to him and woke him saying, "Save us, Lord, we are going down!" And he said to them, "Why are you so frightened, you who have so little faith?" And then he stood up and rebuked the winds and the sea; and all was calm again.' (Matthew 8:24–26) His faith overcame their fear. He believed and trusted that God his Father was looking after them. His faith taught them a lesson about the *indispensable* importance of faith in their lives and mission. On another occasion, when they failed to cast a devil out of a young boy and asked Jesus why they had failed, he answered, 'Because you have little faith. I tell you solemnly, if your faith were the size of a mustard seed you will say to this mountain, "Move from here to there", and it will move; nothing will be impossible for you.' (Matthew 17:19–20)

Faith and healing were essentially linked together. Jesus believed that his Father answered him whenever he asked in faith. The same holds true today because Jesus has promised to be with his followers always in his presence and power (Matthew 18:19; Mark 16: 17–18). Whenever Jesus was asked to heal anyone and he discerned in prayer that this was what his Father wanted him to do, he did it. He *trusted* his Father completely with the end result. The raising of Lazarus from the dead is a perfect example of his prayer of faith and trust in his Father. ' "Father, I thank you for hearing my prayer. I knew indeed that you always hear me, but I speak for the sake of all these who stand round me, so that they may believe it was you who sent me." When he had said this, he cried in a loud voice, "Lazarus, here! Come out!" The dead man came out, his hands and feet bound with bands of stuff and a cloth round his face. Jesus said to them, "Unbind him, let him go free." ' (John 11:41–44) Jesus thanked his Father in trust for already answering his prayer *before* Lazarus came out of the tomb. His faith and trust in his Father's work would demonstrate not only that God our Father was with him in a very special way, but it would also help those standing round to believe in God and to praise him for his glorious works. Trust is the other side of the coin of faith and, like faith, it too is indispensable to healing.

Jesus was a man of *prayer.* This was the source and strength of his healing ministry. After a full day's healing in Capernaum, where 'the whole town came crowding round the door' the next morning, long before dawn, Jesus 'got up and left the house, and went off to a lonely place and prayed there' (Mark 1: 35). All his healing flowed from prayer. Whenever Jesus prayed to his Father in faith and trust his request was always granted. He wanted his followers to have the same confidence in the power of prayer to elicit a positive response from God the Father. 'Ask, and it will be given to you; search, and you will find; knock, and the door will be opened to you. For the one who asks *always* receives; the one who searches *always* finds; the one who knocks will *always* have the door opened to him.' (Matthew 7:7–8) In our prayer for the healing of others, we too are healed in our wounded selves. Jesus is ultimately the healer of all those who believe in him, 'because through his wounds you have been healed' (1 Peter 2:24).

Jesus suffered for us and in his suffering he not only identifies with us, but heals us. Jesus is the *wounded healer.* 'In Jesus, the Son of God, we have the supreme high priest . . . For it is not as if we had a high priest who was incapable of feeling our weaknesses with us; but we have one who has been tempted in every way that we are, though he is without sin. Let us be confident, then, in approaching the throne of grace, that we shall have mercy from him and find grace when we are in need of help.' (Hebrews 4:14–16) As a wounded healer, Jesus was sensitive to the pain of those round him. He was *compassionate* because he had experienced in his own person the wounds of a violent world and people who would not accept his healing and teaching. He chose not to remain aloof from our pain, but identified with it even to the point of laying down his life for our sake: 'The Son of Man came not to be served but to serve, and to give his life as a ransom for many' (Matthew 20:28); 'A man can have no greater love than to lay down his life for his friends. You are my friends' (John 15:13–14).

The ransom for our healing as persons is the wounds of Jesus. He never tried to explain suffering, but saw it as part of the pattern of our lives because we are all wounded by sin. He raised suffering to a higher level by accepting it as an expression of love for his Father, to whose will he surrendered his life. By his example he became a source of inner strength, purpose and peace to all those who suffer in the shadow of his cross. 'All you who pass this way, look and see: is any sorrow like the sorrow that afflicts me' (Lamentations 1:12).

> As he drew near and came in sight of the city [Jerusalem] he shed tears over it and said, 'If you in your turn had only understood on this day the message of peace! But, alas, it is hidden from your eyes . . . because you did not recognise the moment of your visitation.' (Luke 19:41–42, 44)

Today's world needs the witness of Christ's healing power, which is still with those who believe in him and are called to follow him in this ministry of healing.

3

Jesus and Fear

Jesus lived in terrifying conditions. His life from begin-ning to end was set against a background of fear and violence. He had to come to terms with all these circum-stances in his mind and heart. His constant teaching and encouragement to his disciples, especially after his resur-rection, was 'Have courage; do not be afraid.' He certainly practised what he preached. His life of healing and rec-onciliation by which he restored peaceful relationships between us and God, ourselves and our neighbours, and within ourselves, was challenged on all sides; to put it in simple language, his life was turbulent. If anyone should have yielded to fear then it was Jesus. He would have done so were it not for his *faith*, a fact often overlooked by many of those who study and write about his life. They see him only as the Son of God, forgetting that he was also truly human. I believe that his *humanity*, and the way he coped with fear in his own life, is an example for you and me to follow when fear threatens to take us over and control us. He was not aloof from the sufferings and fears of those around him; he was one of them, and in his physical wounds and emotional conflicts, he experienced what they did, perhaps even more so, because he was so sensi-tive and conscious of his mission to heal fear in others!

In the battle with fear within himself, Jesus is our model of how to cope with fear in our own lives when crises occur. In the face of violent opposition, he was not immune from fear just because he was the Son of God.

If he had been, then he would be less than human since fear is part and parcel of our damaged human nature. Jesus is one with us precisely because he is human. In his writings St Paul constantly reminds us that Jesus so identified himself with our human condition that he was like us in everything but sin. 'His state was divine, yet he did not cling to his equality with God but emptied himself to assume the condition of a slave, and became as men are; and being as all men are, he was humbler yet, even to accepting death, death on a cross.' (Philippians 2:6–8) Jesus was, like you and me, subject to all the weaknesses and temptations of a humanity alienated from God. He was subjected to fear and it is a great help to us to understand how he reacted to it, especially in the Garden of Gethsemane. When he was faced with a crisis he did not find it easy to cope and neither will we. His conquering of fear as a person gives us renewed courage and hope in our journey through life when at times we too are overwhelmed by fear and do not know how to deal with it.

All the words and actions of Jesus have an inherent healing power for us against the forces of fear, but none more so than the events and his reactions to them during his agony in Gethsemane. They show clearly how he coped with the greatest fear in his life. I have found that reflection on this dark night of fear in Our Lord's life has given me helpful insights into his life as well as my own, and shown me how to cope with fear when I have to face it. The over-emphasis on the divinity of Jesus by many pious writers has so stifled his humanity in our understanding of him that we can easily forget how real was his fear, especially during his agony in Gethsemane. His fear then was so real that 'his sweat fell to the ground like great drops of blood' (Luke 22:44). He prayed in the Garden of Gethsemane to be let off his sufferings. 'My Father,' he said 'if it is possible let this cup pass me by' (Matthew 26:39). Yet the cup of suffering did not pass him by.

If we try to place ourselves in his situation then perhaps we can begin to understand how the prospect of his crucifixion must have made him so afraid that he was tempted to give in completely to his fear. If he had done so – and there was always that possibility, if he was truly human – then how could we even begin to hope to conquer fear in our own lives?

'During his life on earth, [Jesus] offered up prayer and entreaty, aloud and in silent tears, to the one who had the power to save him out of death, and he submitted so humbly that his prayer was heard. Although he was Son, he learnt to obey through suffering; but having been made perfect, he became for all who obey him the source of eternal salvation' (Hebrews 5:7–9). Because he was human, Jesus shows us that it is only to be expected that, as a result of our damaged human nature, there will be times in our life when fear will try to take us over. Fear is a result of our damaged nature. But like him, when we are no longer afraid of being afraid then we can begin truly to appreciate and conquer fear within ourselves. Just as the alcoholic has to admit to his alcoholism before he can be cured, so we need to acknowledge our fear as the first step to changing the direction of our lives.

From his birth to his death Jesus was surrounded by people who were victims of obsessive fear. Jerusalem was a city of rumour and intrigue. The people's religion had become horribly mixed up with politics. Jesus was trapped between synagogue and state. His words were open to misinterpretation, especially when he spoke of 'freedom' or 'a kingdom'. In the proclamation of his message, he had to choose his words and timing carefully. This was one of the main reasons why he spoke to his listeners in the form of stories. He was caught up in the vortex of violence and fear which such a situation breeds. It was as if his life had unlocked the forces of evil.

Even though Jesus' 'kingdom' was not of this world, Herod had innocent children slaughtered, because of him, in order to protect his throne. Jesus preached 'freedom' to a people who lived not so much under the yoke of Roman imperialism as under the burden of bigotry and observance of petty religious laws. His teaching was too near the bone, too prophetic, for the people of his time. If they wanted him to remain silent then they had no option but to kill him. If ever a man should have been filled with fear then surely it was Jesus. But no one could ever take away his inner peace which was so obviously his hidden source of strength and courage all through his life, even during his dying on the cross.

By his example and actions Jesus came to set people free from fear so that they could live in deep inner peace. Yet for such a peaceful man, he seemed to touch off hidden forces of bigotry and frustration everywhere, until finally, in Jerusalem, the people gathered in the city for a religious feast suddenly disintegrated into a rabble shouting for his blood. It was a straightforward choice – Jesus or Barabbas, peace or violence. He had only preached peace and a rabble always chooses violence. From Pilate and the Sanhedrin down to the man in the street, they were all afraid of whom he might be – 'So you are a king then?' – and of what he might do – 'He said he would destroy the temple.' Their fears played on his words and twisted them at his trial. Fear won the day when they crucified peace on a hill called Golgotha.

From the moment he was captured by the soldiers until his death, Jesus was the most calm and controlled person amid all the ugly scenes that shook Jerusalem to the foundations. It was as if he alone, among leaders of state and religion, preserved his dignity and sense of purpose. What kept him going when most people would have cracked under the strain? Was he showing himself to be a God who was not affected by fearful, puny people who were looking for a scapegoat? The answer, quite simply, is that he was showing himself to be *a man of faith* who had come face to face with fear within himself and had

conquered it. After his agony in the Garden of Gethsemane he was ready for anything that people could do to
him. His fear was under control. His real trial was not
before Pilate, but in the Garden of Gethsemane when he
conquered fear. There he had reached his decision and
remained at peace within himself. It will help us to understand his inner power of peace if we examine in some
detail the circumstances of his encounter with himself in
the darkness of that garden.

Jesus had all the symptoms of someone under great
stress and one could describe him as being on *the verge of
a nervous breakdown*. He was tempted to throw in the towel
and cede victory to the massive forces arraigned against
him. In human terms, he could not win and the thought
must have occurred to him to slip away from all the
violence and wait for a more opportune time to preach
his message when things had quietened down. In the
meantime, he could carry on his wonderful work of healing. After all, he was only thirty-three years of age, with
much of his life before him. This form of rationalising,
while human, did not take into account his Father's will.
In prayer, he learns more clearly what has to be and he
surrenders lovingly. This is his moment of crisis and the
moment of truth.

In him we all see ourselves as we grapple with the
problems of *faith* and *fear.* We compare our problems with
his. We too have to ask ourselves the question of why we
are placed under stress and tension in particular situations. 'Why us, Lord?' we ask. Jesus is a man in agony
who has finally arrived at crisis point and at the moment
of greatest trial his faith in God his Father carries him
through. He told his captors, 'This is your hour; this is
the reign of darkness' (Luke 22:53). In fact, it was his
glorious hour when faith conquers fear and light overcomes the darkness. We will never conquer fear or come
to know ourselves unless we pray. Fear comes to us all. It
is in prayer that the great decisions in life are taken, once

we allow faith to cancel out fear. What Jesus has done, we know that in faith we can do. We are never alone when we turn to God in prayer and in him we find our new strength.

Here is how Matthew's gospel describes the 'crisis situation':

> Then Jesus came with them to a small estate called Gethsemane; and he said to his disciples, 'Stay here while I go over there to pray.' He took Peter and the two sons of Zebedee with him. And sadness came over him, and great distress. Then he said to them, 'My soul is sorrowful to the point of death. Wait here and keep awake with me.' And going on a little further he fell on his face and prayed. *'My Father,'* he said, *'if it is possible, let this cup pass me by. Nevertheless, let it be as you, not I, would have it.'* He came back to the disciples and found them sleeping, and he said to Peter, 'So you had not the strength to keep awake with me one hour? You should be awake, and praying not to be put to the test. The spirit is willing, but the flesh is weak.' Again, a second time, he went away and prayed: *'My Father'* he said *'if this cup cannot pass by without my drinking it, your will be done!'* And he came back again and found them sleeping, their eyes were so heavy. Leaving them there, he went away again and prayed for the third time, repeating the same words. Then he came back to the disciples and said to them, *'You can sleep now and take your rest . . . My betrayer is already close at hand.'* (Matthew 26:36–46)

What do we learn about coping with fear within ourselves when we study the behaviour of Jesus during his time of trial by self-examination in that lonely Garden of Gethsemane? Because he was under extreme pressure, Jesus took three of his closest followers with him to keep him company. By his example he was showing us that you cannot share your deepest fears with just anyone; the ones you choose have to be special to you, people you can trust. It is easier to overcome fear when you can talk to someone who understands you. We all need the comforting contact of friends, even if it is only to know that they are physically near us. They may be able to offer no other kind of help, because basically the problem within us can only be solved by ourselves before God alone. No one else can solve our really big problems for us: we have to face up to the crisis ourselves and grow from it as real persons. I know that in any major crisis of my life, it is when I have given myself time and space to reflect and pray that I have found the answer which had always been there deep within myself – I just had to find it. The most difficult person to live with is yourself.

In Gethsemane it was a time of trial for Jesus 'and sadness came over him, and great distress'. We discover who we really are in moments of great joy or deep sorrow. They are sent to make us grow as real people. Jesus shared his crisis with those whom he could really trust. He confided in them, hoping that they would understand what he was going through: '*My soul is sorrowful to the point of death.*' He was so distressed that his sorrow overpowered him – a typical example of someone who sees no way out of the dilemma in which he finds himself. Is this the end or only the beginning? In fact while it was near the end of his own physical life, it was only the beginning of his glorious new life in the world. When everything else seems lost, we discover ourselves in a new way. It is when we think we have lost God that we are nearest to finding him and being found by him. When fear threatens, God seems far away even though he is never closer at hand.

All Jesus asked of his closest friends was: 'Wait here and keep awake with me.' They were his 'moral' support. If Jesus was willing to depend on others, then surely we should not be too proud to ask for the help and healing of others in times of need. Even though we have to solve the problem ourselves and make the decision alone, it is encouraging to know that others care about what happens to us. Jesus had spent his whole public life helping others and now it was his turn to receive their help. It is important to realise that it is blessed to receive as well as to give. Jesus proved that he was fully human by his urgent plea for assistance while he faced his future in prayer. He reminds us that it is not weakness for us to seek help from others in our moments of crisis. It is false courage and pride to think that we can cope alone. It seems strange, however, to think of Jesus being so afraid that he sought the help of others, especially when we remember that time and again in his public life Jesus demanded total dedication from his followers. He never compromised on the hardships of following him:

> 'If anyone wants to be a follower of mine, let him renounce himself and take up his cross every day and follow me. For anyone who wants to save his life will lose it; but anyone who loses his life for my sake, that man will save it. What gain, then, is it for a man to have won the whole world and to have lost or ruined his very self?' (Luke 9:23–5)

> As they travelled along they met a man on the road who said to him, 'I will follow you wherever you go.' Jesus answered, 'Foxes have holes and the birds of the air have nests, but the Son of Man has nowhere to lay his head.'
> Another to whom he said, 'Follow me', replied, 'Let me go and bury my father first.' But he answered, 'Leave the dead to bury their dead; your duty is to go and spread the news of the kingdom of God.'
> Another said, 'I will follow you, sir, but first let me go and say good-bye to my people at home.' Jesus said to him, 'Once the hand is laid on the plough, no one who looks back is fit for the kingdom of God.' (Luke 9:57–62)

In Gethsemane the boot was now firmly on the other foot. Jesus was faced with the question of how much he loved his Father. He had asked total love of others, now he proved himself the perfect leader who followed his own instruction. He still asked, 'If it is possible, let this cup pass from me.' But it did not pass from him and he had to drink it to the dregs. We too in our lives preach the gospel of total love for and faith in God, but there come times of crisis when we are put to the test. A whole lifetime often finds its climax in a single decision affecting our life and faith. I know literally hundreds of people in my pastoral experience who have given up everything to follow Jesus, turning their backs on wealth and security, power and privilege because it meant living a way of life which ran counter to their faith. Their response was total surrender. This is the stuff of which saints are made. They are our cloud of witnesses in heaven and on earth of the power of faith against all odds. Faith was their precious jewel for which they gave up everything.

The test of faith for Jesus came that evening in Gethsemane. His faith had been built up over the years to equip him to deal with his moment of trial. So, too, in our own experience we find that our faith of years is tested in a situation, perhaps not of our own making. We can pray, like Jesus, for the cup to pass by, but when it is not possible, we willingly accept the decision with all its consequences. We are prepared to die for our faith because without it life would not be worth living. Fear has no power over us once we are prepared to live a life of faith which even death itself cannot conquer. If we live faith-filled lives there is no room in our spirits for fear which turns us away from God.

In our moments of crisis we may often find that we are let down by those from whom we would rightly expect help and support. It was the same with Jesus in his time of trial. When he returned to his disciples he 'found them sleeping, their eyes were so heavy'. They had, in a sense, failed him and so Jesus comes to his decision alone before his Father. Jesus tells us, by his example, that no one can solve the problems that trouble the deepest parts of our soul, but God alone in our encounter with him. No one can solve another's problems which touch the 'deep', inner soul of a person's conscience. It is only God who shows us the way to an authentic answer. The building up of faith and trust in God our Father who loves us and will never let us down, especially in our darkest hour, is one of the most important messages in our El Shaddai ministry. We support people in crisis so that they will not lose faith in themselves or in God. They may be faced with the knowledge that they are seriously ill or they may have suffered a bereavement. In those times we are one with them in prayer that they will come through their trial and suffering with dignity and courage. Like Jesus, who said to Peter, 'I have prayed for you, that your faith may not fail' (Luke 22:32), we pray that their belief in God's power to help them will never waver. Sometimes we have to stand by and watch them struggle within themselves in their agony when faith and fear are locked in combat. It costs us dearly when we watch the struggle and feel so inadequate and helpless, unable to do anything to relieve their pain. In their suffering we find a compassion within ourselves which we surrender to God if we are to remain at peace, so that we can help those we love in their agony. In our agony we should ask God for positive help; we should not lie down fatalistically under our burden. This is not how Jesus acted in his moment of crisis, when he prayed: 'My Father, if it is possible, let this cup pass me by. Nevertheless, let it be as you, not I, would have it.' The prayer of Jesus is a prayer of faith. He knew all his life that God believed in him, but now it was his turn to believe totally in God. He could not see the answer or a way out of his situation, but he was prepared to surrender everything, including his life. He did not want to die, but his trust in God was absolute: 'Let it be as you, not I,

would have it.' We often pray, 'my will be done and yours
only when it coincides with mine'. But we are not praying
the prayer of true faith, the prayer of someone who
places God's will at the centre of his thoughts. Jesus really
meant what he said when he left the final outcome to his
Father.

How did Jesus manage to do this? The simple answer
is that he was Father-orientated. Even in the midst of all
his anxiety, God was still his Father. He is ours too. His
ways are not ours and we do not know all the answers. In
times of crisis we hand over our fears to him, believing
and trusting in his loving purpose for us. The dynamic
force directing the life of Jesus was his love for his Father
and for us whom he came to redeem – a love 'that looks
on tempests and is never shaken'. A loving faith does not
always have a ready answer, but is prepared to listen to
God who will provide the answer. Faith which has all the
answers is no faith at all. Abraham did not have the answer
when he climbed the mountain, prepared to sacrifice his
son Isaac; that is why he is called 'our father in faith'.
When Isaac asked his father the question, 'Here are the
fire and the wood, but where is the lamb for the burnt
offering?', Abraham answered, 'My son, God himself will
provide the lamb for the burnt offering' (Genesis 22:7–8).
God did provide the offering in the person of Abraham's
only son. Jesus in Gethsemane is our brother in faith, and
those who say that he knew all the answers to his life
detract from his living faith which still called God 'my
Father' in the agony of his greatest trial.

Jesus needed all the faith he could muster during his
'crisis' and when he was put to the test he was not found
wanting. Theologians in the past have not stressed sufficiently the humanity of Jesus nor highlighted enough
his faith as an example to us all. Too often they have so
over-emphasised his divinity that they have almost ignored
his humanity, thus defeating the whole purpose and
meaning of the incarnation. Jesus has often been depicted

as 'too holy to be real' or else made into such a superman that his way of life completely transcends ours. In this false approach to Jesus we tend to forget that he is one of us and so completely identify him with God that he is God and nothing else. I believe that Jesus as a man had a very special personal faith through his open response to his Father. He loved God with a total human love. He is our model of faith, trust and love. In Gethsemane he suffered the pain of total surrender in love to his Father. For me, suffering only has meaning when we grow in love because of it. Sometimes I do not understand suffering but I accept it in faith, believing that God my Father is sending it to me because he loves me. It was this approach to God which helped Jesus to face all the agony of his rejection and crucifixion. If one can use the words loosely, he came through his suffering 'a better person'. He probably did not grasp the full significance of his agony but he was willing to undergo it because of the love which was part of his living faith. In times of crisis, faith is more important than knowledge of the final outcome.

This emphasis on a *living faith* is much more real as well as being more relevant to us than any ill-founded piety which would depict Jesus as someone who knew everything always. If that were the case, then to what purpose was all the suffering in the Garden of Gethsemane? It would have been a sham with no meaning for us, as if Jesus were saying to himself, 'This will soon be over, so for a little while I shall just have to grin and bear it.' This minimising of Jesus' faith is destructive of the gospels which accepted the *full humanity* of the person before their eyes. John knew about whom he was writing: 'Something which has existed since the beginning, that we have heard, and we have seen with our own eyes; that we have watched and touched with our hands; the Word, who is life – this is our subject. That life was made visible; we saw it and we are giving our testimony' (1 John 1:1–2). Jesus, the man of faith in his time of crisis, encourages us to be the same. How tragic it is when those in a crisis of suffering have little or no faith on which to draw. This to me is the supreme tragedy. It seems a meaningless agony with little or no sign of any maturing of the person on trial. Suffering is necessary for us to grow in an awareness of ourselves, but, where there is no faith, then suffering is indeed futile: it is like planting vines in a desert.

Jesus, in his living, loving faith, rises up from prayer and is completely at peace within himself. He has come to terms with suffering and is prepared for whatever is still to come. He has been through the valley of darkness, so what evil should he fear? God is with and in him. He is refreshed and invigorated with new strength to face his enemies who are close at hand. 'You have prepared a banquet for me in the sight of my foes' (Psalm 23). Jesus loves his Father and any love worth the name involves suffering. When we come through our pain we will view the world and everything in it in a new light. It was as if before we were only half-seeing everything but now, when we look from the hill-top of faith beyond the valley of suffering, we will have a clearer and more far-reaching vision. This is always the case with people of faith who have suffered: they see their desert as God's garden where in a special way they have experienced his presence and love.

From this point on, throughout his trial and death Jesus has a mysterious calmness and courage which is difficult for his enemies to understand. He had died completely to himself in the garden and his peace of soul is something which no one can take from him. It was as if when the Roman soldiers beat him in the courtyard they were battering futilely at a stout door which would not yield. His silence before the priests was more than an eloquent defence; it was a hymn of praise for his Father whom he knew could deliver him. He walked in the light of his Father's love. It is not surprising that the Roman centurion, who saw many criminals die on a cross, screaming for mercy or vengeance, realised that Jesus was different: 'In truth this man was a Son of God' (Mark 15:39). Jesus lived a new life, as it were, after his agony in the garden. He had been through his trial within himself and with God; a trial of hate by men, however gruesome, was nothing by comparison. Jesus was truly alive and his love shone clearly on those around him, if only they would look. The soldiers could kill his body, but as a person he belonged to his Father. We too can achieve this serenity once we rid ourselves of a fear which tries to control us. We will find that our crisis has changed us; we have grown as persons. This alone is the point of suffering. It challenges our faith and love in a God who never ceases to love us.

What was the extent of Jesus' fear? We will never know, but we can say that despite his fear he won through as a man of faith and love. He could, without sin, have refused to die. Many people think that he could not have done anything else but obey because he was God: this is quite false. As a man he was so in love with his Father and with us that he was prepared to undergo anything, whatever the cost to himself. He was free. He had no special means of avoiding the crisis, so he was just like you and me in our trials and suffering. He conquered fear in himself and invites us to do the same. He speaks to us in our moment of crisis: 'I know what it feels like to be tempted to throw in the towel, but please remember I am with you in your agony, I went through my crisis, and my victory is your hope. Keep your eyes fixed on me. Whatever you may suffer, I have been there before you. Come, follow me.'

In our El Shaddai ministry of healing, we have found that this emphasis on the humanity and faith of Jesus has been immeasurably powerful in helping thousands of people to conquer fear in their own lives. Once we ask the question 'Jesus were you ever afraid?', knowing that he was, then immediately the sufferings and faith of Christ become real to people. They identify with him, because they appreciate what he has been through. It is only a short step in faith for them to realise that he is with them in their sufferings and that he is praying for them that their faith will not fail them in their moment of crisis. Without the meeting of fear and faith in the humanity of Christ then there is little hope for us in our healing ministry to help people relate our fear to his. He is our genuine model and anchor.

Throughout this book, as in the healing ministry of El Shaddai, several important points are stressed:

- Jesus was not only God, but was also perfectly human.
- Fear is part of our human condition.
- During his life, Jesus struggled with fear which tried to control him.
- His fear was conquered by faith.
- Faith controls fear so that we can grow through each crisis.
- We need to share with others whom we can trust, but ultimately we conquer our fear when we turn to God.
- God, our Father of love and light, will not abandon us to darkness of fear when we pray to him in faith and trust the outcome to him.
- However close we may be to fearful people and pray for their healing, it is their personal encounter with God their loving Father which will ultimately rid them of their fear and bring them inner peace.

When Jesus rose from the dead, his message to his followers was one of peace. He repeated his advice to them time and again: 'Do not be afraid.' He knew only too well what fear was, but he had surrendered himself and his life to his Father. When we are in our agony we may ask him, 'Were you afraid, Lord?' He will answer, 'Yes, and I conquered it. Like death it has no sting. I am with you now. I am praying for you that your faith will not fail you. When you win through you will stand by my side and together we will bury fear forever.'

4

Fear of God

The basis of our El Shaddai ministry is our unshakeable belief that God is our Father who loves us every moment of every day in every situation. He knows who and what we are. He takes us as we are because we can come to him in no other way. *He always heals us.* He brings us the inner peace of Jesus his Son which conquers fear because it comes from love – not our love of God but his love for us. Love and fear cannot exist together: they are incompatible. If we want peace of mind and heart then all we have to do is to allow God's love to flow into us. It is a stream of living water which brings us hope, joy and a new vision of who we are and what life is all about. We think positively by removing the blockage which fear causes in our lives. Knowing that God loves us, we call on him to help us carry our burdens. He will answer. Jesus said, 'Come to me, all you who labour and are overburdened, and I will give you rest. Shoulder my yoke and learn from me, for I am gentle and humble in heart, and you will find rest for your souls. Yes, my yoke is easy and my burden light.' (Matthew 11:28–30) Simon of Cyrene helped Jesus to carry his cross. No one carries his cross alone. A burden shared is a burden lightened. When Christ is with us then we have nothing to fear. All is well, and all will be well.

Far too many so-called Christians are high on fear and low on love. They are afraid of everything and everyone, especially God. The paradox is that Christians by their

calling are meant to love God. Jesus said, 'You must love
the Lord your God with all your heart, with all your soul,
and with all your mind. This is the greatest and the first
commandment.' (Matthew 22:38) So many people have
false ideas of God. He is not the loving Father of the
gospel preached and lived by Jesus Christ, but a vengeful
God instilled in them by false teaching. Yet the most
important thing in life for us as Christians is to *allow* God
to love us as our Father. If we want to be free to be
ourselves then we must allow God to be free to be himself;
we must not block his love or have false ideas about what
he is like. The gospel of Jesus is so full of God's love for
us as a Father that it is impossible for us to be Christians
and not allow God as he really is into our lives as someone
with whom we can, and want to, share everything. It is his
love for us which dispels our fear, his care which prevents
us from worrying unduly about our lives.

> That is why I am telling you not to worry about your
> life and what you are to eat, nor about your body and
> how you are to clothe it. Surely life means more than
> food, and the body more than clothing! Look at the
> birds in the sky. They do not sow or reap or gather into
> barns; yet your heavenly Father feeds them. Are you not
> worth much more than they are? Can any of you, for
> all his worrying, add one single cubit to his span of
> life? . . . So do not worry; do not say, 'What are we to
> eat? What are we to drink? How are we to be clothed?'
> It is the pagans who set their hearts on all these things.
> Your heavenly Father knows you need them all. Set your
> hearts on his kingdom first, and on his righteousness,
> and all these other things will be given you as well.
> (Matthew 6:25–33)

And yet we do not trust God with our lives. We worry
needlessly about many things so that we live in an atmosphere of perpetual anxiety and fear. Why are we so fearful? The answer is simple and basic to Christian healing.

If we are fearful of God as Christians it is because we have not experienced God's love for us as his children. We may claim to know all about him as the God of love, but we do not know, experience him as a loving God. He is not real for us as a loving Father but seen as 'someone out there', if indeed he exists at all except in our social moralising way of looking at him which we call faith, but which is often thinly disguised fear hiding under the mantel of religion. Faith dispels fear, whereas religion often fosters its presence and growth within the life of its victim. In our healing sessions we encounter people of fear as numerous as victims in a casualty hospital. The gospel of love is the blood transfusion which brings new life of freedom and joy. I cannot over-emphasise the destructive force of fear which is prevalent once we probe beneath the surface of religion masquerading as faith. The saddest thing which I experience in our healing sessions is the number of people who look on God as someone who fills them with irrational fear and foreboding.

If we analyse our fear of God we will have to acknowledge that basically the reason why we do not love him is because we do not know him, or what he wants for us. We reject, in fact, the 'God' who does not exist. We are afraid of what loving God involves. We want to remain ourselves, and we fear that God would want to change us, or those we love, if we committed ourselves to him. *We are afraid that, in healing, God will want us to live his way and not ours.* This is the most prevalent fear, and like a polluted stream it runs into every aspect of life and healing. Healing changes our accustomed way of life, and we fear change so much that we even want to protect others from healing because we want them to remain as they are. Strange as it may seem, I have come across cases where parents themselves do not want their handicapped children to be physically healed by God because this would mean a change, not so much in their children's lives, but in their own.

Maureen's parents came to our healing session in Ennis in Ireland, and they brought her with them ostensibly for physical healing. She was a severe case of spina bifida and yet she was brimful of laughter and sharing. Her parents were frightened of what would happen once our healing team had ministered to her. Her mother wrote to me later about her own feelings:

'We brought Maureen to Lourdes several times and we received great spiritual blessings there but gradually it dawned on me that I did not look or pray for a physical miracle. We loved her as she was and we were afraid that if she were physically healed her life and ours would change. We were scared that night at the healing session in church. As you approached Maureen, I prayed 'God, don't let her be healed.' Then when I heard you speak so gently to her, and ask her to pray for you and your work in the ministry of healing, I realised how selfish I was. As you knelt before her and asked her to lay hands on your head, I felt all my fear disappear. I said to God, 'Whatever you want, Lord, whatever you want.' Of course it was my husband and I who were healed of our fear of change. Maureen is just as beautiful and happy, and we are now totally free to let God have his way with her and us.'

As in the case of Maureen's parents, so often we too hold on to what we have. We are afraid that God will be selfish and demanding of us in his love. Yet if God is pure love then his relationship with us will be totally unselfish and creative. *He puts our needs first, and respects our freedom.* He wants our response to him to be the same, even though it will take a lifetime to grow. When we surrender to him in love, a little timidly at first, we will begin to shed our fears like a child who comes out of darkness into a wonderful new world of light.

Perhaps we stay out of the waters of deep faith for fear of drowning. But isn't that what the waters of baptism were meant to be – a drowning of the old self and a new birth in Christ? We die in baptism to all our fears and these we bury with Christ in the old tomb of self, so that we can emerge as a new creation. 'You have been taught that when we were baptised in Christ Jesus we were baptised in his death; in other words, when we were baptised we went into the tomb with him and joined him in death, so that as Christ was raised from the dead by the Father's glory, we too might live a new life.' (Romans 6:3–4)

If we knew God as our Father we would, of course, trust him and become the kind of person he wants us to be; we would want to do this no matter what the cost to ourselves. This is how Jesus lived. In the final analysis, however, we do not trust ourselves to God's loving care for our destiny because we find it difficult to believe that such a love exists anywhere in the world. It seems too good to be true since so many things seem to happen by chance. Yet God gets up an hour earlier than fate every morning! Our crisis in growth as individuals is a crisis of faith and hope. We do not believe in God as our father and that is why we do not trust him. We prefer to manage our own lives and keep our hands on the helm, so that at least we can be sure of our future. We do not even begin to get a glimmer of what the word 'God' means because we have never plumbed the depths of human love. We have not experienced the joy and pain of loving another for himself or herself alone. If the word 'love' means little to us, then God has no meaning. Husbands and wives in true married love give to the other totally, and would not have it otherwise. As soon as they decide to give only as much as they receive, then their marriage is heading for the dangerous rocks of selfishness and destruction. We have not lived out, as Christians, our top priority – the true meaning of generous love – and this defect more than any other is the reason why people today are not prepared to believe in God. Yet if they are honest with themselves deep down in their hearts they are more impressed by lives than dogmas.

Fearful people do not believe in themselves and cannot comprehend how anyone could believe in them, least of all God. *What we need today, then, is not so much a belief in God but a belief that God believes in us.* What is the effect of this truth? 'A new creature,' says St Paul – a free man, free of fear and free for love. A person full of the juice and joy of living, someone transformed who is really a son and not a slave; a man at one with himself because he is saturated by the truth of the gospel, which uplifts him and gives a new dimension to his life. God has also made us free. He handed over to us the human management of his world and his Church, and he will never take them back from us. This is the staggering price we pay for daring to call ourselves Christians. Yet many fearful people feel they are a big disappointment to God and to themselves. John was a typical example of this approach to life. Emotionally his personality was crippled.

'All my life I messed everything up. Whatever I touched seemed to come apart in my hands. I seemed to have a curse on me. Even when I was very young I was afraid to volunteer to do anything in case I got it wrong. As I grew up I tried to form human relationships but I was the one who just could not keep the friendship going. So people got tired of me and I don't blame them. I used to go to church every week but soon felt isolated. I was afraid to let people know what I was feeling deep inside so I kept myself to myself. Soon my prayers to God became filled with fear. How could he believe in me since I was such a failure? I haven't prayed for years now except for the odd time now and then. But I don't think he likes me, and will take me to task for my wasted life. I fear him more than anyone or anything else.'

John has been to many of our healing sessions and gradually his fear has been healed. We helped to show him that he was not a failure, and that no matter what he thought of himself, God loved him as his Father and had confidence in him. John had to be healed of hurtful memories, false guilt and a thousand and one other things. In fact, he was more sinned against than sinning. No one had really helped him to change his own lack of appreciation of himself and guide him into concentrating on God the Father who loved him always. Today John is a different person. Even his physical appearance has changed. He has a new, more fulfilling job, and above all he helps others. He no longer lives within a self he had come to hate.

Fear will invariably arise, even though we may not recognise it as such, whenever *we substitute the external trappings of religion for a living faith in a loving God.* We may come to look on God as a judge who watches our every action and notes everything we do wrong, so that sin and fear, instead of grace and love, become the main factors in our lives. But how did we get this false notion of God? The blame lies in the way religion was taught in previous ages, a way which has done so much harm to people's spiritual lives by its unbalanced emphasis on the wrath of God who will punish with untold tortures those who break his laws. Medieval art proves the point. No denomination is free from this charge of building up complexes which paralysed people and gave rise to all sorts of abuses of true faith. Religion was related not to life but to death! Can we honestly say that our memories of religious services in our youth filled us with joy, or was Sunday service a bore which we attended out of duty rather than choice? What was your experience? I can only tell you about mine.

For many years my life was dominated by the fear of falling into mortal sin which would automatically cut me off from God. I saw God as a judge, and I was literally terrified of hell about which I had many nightmares. Justification was achieved by personal effort so that life became increasingly full of tensions and anxieties. The big sin, of course, was sex, and the sermon which attracted maximum attendance during a parish mission was the one which dealt with the evils of 'company keeping'. I have heard sermons preached which made me feel that my sins would have brought a blush to the cheeks of even the most hardened sinners of Sodom and Gomorra. God became such a kill-joy that I compartmentalised religion until gradually it was reduced to a one-hour exercise to be undertaken on Sundays in my best clothes. It had nothing to do with life or being human. 'The fear of the Lord is the beginning of wisdom' (Proverbs 1:7) was quoted to me time and again. I realised that 'It was a dreadful thing to fall into the hands of the living God' (Hebrews 10:31). So I stayed out of his reach as much as possible. Whatever the truth about heaven, I certainly knew there was a hell. I was happy because, in some strange way, I did not allow religion to dominate my waking hours or enter my leisure time. Religion at school was learned by rote, to be quoted at length in the same mechanical way as our multiplication tables when we were questioned as to why we believed. It was mainly an intellectual exercise and the approach too apologetic, unreal and cold. I cannot say that God was ever real to me at school, even though the Catholic Church in the person of the priest loomed so large in my life. I am sure this was not the intention of my teachers, but it was in fact what they achieved by their teaching and attitude. They never let me forget that I was a Catholic and a member of the largest Christian denomination in the world. I could only be saved as a Catholic and the unpardonable crime of rejecting my faith would bring shame on my entire family.

I was not yet converted to a notion of a loving God even though my parents were so obviously fulfilled as Catholics. I felt in some tangible way, which I could not analyse, that there must be something special in the Catholic faith because of how much it meant to them. They were happy and the secret lay in the fact that their religion was part and parcel of everything they were and did. I did not want to hurt them by opting out, even though

I knew in my teens that many of my contemporaries had lapsed from the faith without any apparent evil consequences. But what did they lapse from? I believe it was from a parody and a caricature of who God really is. They did not in fact reject God, but the monster who was presented to them. All this fear and wrong motivation has now changed for me, but there are still large numbers of people of all denominations who carry this image to the grave. Only recently I prayed with an old woman suffering from a terminal disease who was afraid of death precisely because of her wrong spiritual formation. She and I went through mental torture as I tried to unravel with her the knots which she had got herself into over the years. God revealed to her the wonders of his love as she lived at peace in his presence the last few days of her life.

Today my attitude to my Christian faith has undergone a complete change brought about by the power of the Holy Spirit. The spirit of the Risen Christ released me from the tomb of my empty fears so that at last I could call God 'Abba', Father. 'Everyone moved by the Spirit is a son of God. The spirit you received is not the spirit of slaves bringing fear into your lives again; it is the spirit of sons, and it makes us cry out, "Abba, Father!" The Spirit himself and our spirit bear united witness that we are children of God. And if we are children we are heirs as well: heirs of God and coheirs with Christ, sharing his sufferings so as to share his glory.' (Romans 8: 14–17). The great gift Christ gives to you and me is to call God, 'Father'. Christ brought us a freedom of spirit which makes us glad that we are Christians. Our service is real freedom, and when Christ freed us, he meant us to remain free. 'Stand firm, therefore, and do not submit again to the yoke of slavery.' (Galatians 5:1)

Yet sometimes we cannot accept this complete forgiveness of God, and his never-failing love for us. We see and judge ourselves by our own standards of ruthless and unforgiving justice rather than by God's mercy which overcomes our sinfulness because he is aware of our vulnerability in a hostile world. The *feeling of desertion by God and the growth of fear within us that we are abandoned* is the cause of much despair among many people who feel that they cannot cope with the problems that are part and parcel of their everyday living.

Let me give you an example. Jimmy was a typical victim of this false approach to God which had created havoc in his life. He came to help us at our pastoral centre many years ago. He had a severe alcoholic problem and was rebellious against any form of authority. Yet there was no better worker or more peaceful person around the place when he was allowed to get on with his work. He would occasionally suffer a fit of depression, which would result in over-indulgence in 'liquid refreshment' and this led to violence. These bouts invariably happened around Christmas and Easter. Eventually I gained his confidence sufficiently for him to tell me why he became an alcoholic.

'I dropped out of society in my teens,' he said. 'I stopped going to church. I did not care what people thought of me so I lost my job and my self-respect. I became a 'gentleman of the road', getting jobs here and there before moving on. I cut God out of my life. I don't want to talk to him or about him. He has no time for me since I am a lost soul. He deserted me a long time ago. I hate Christmas and Easter because other people are so happy and "holy" and I feel so deserted, so alone. That's why I break out at these times. So you keep your distance from me, Father, and everything will be grand. I don't want any of your converting, I don't want to hear any God talk. It has caused enough trouble in my life.'

Jimmy was my friend; he was a tough nut to crack, but God did it in his own gentle way. Ministering healing to Jimmy was like trying to break in a mountain colt; he kicked out against believing in a loving, forgiving God so many times that I was spiritually black and blue. But there came a moment when he was quiet and still in his mind and heart. We spoke together, heart to heart, and the message came through to him that God had never deserted him, but that he had deserted himself and his own dignity. Today he has fitted exceptionally well into society, even though at times the fear of what happened in the past rears its ugly head in an attempt to fill his life with fear again. At such times, even though it is a struggle, he needs to hang on to his belief that God has forgiven him his past wrongs. Today Jimmy believes that the God who never really deserted him will not only forgive him his past sins, but will not desert him in the future.

There are countless numbers of people who fear God in a way which destroys their vision of life. The most common source of fear is a *false understanding of suffering*. I have seen people accept blindly, as coming from God, the most appalling physical and emotional illnesses which have caused great and, I believe, unnecessary distress to themselves and their loved ones. I pray frequently with young fathers or mothers stricken with terminal diseases, whose main worry is for those they leave behind and the fear of what might happen when they die. They often think that suffering is God's punishment and judgement on them because of their sins. It is hard to persuade these agonised people that God does not love to see them suffer or that he deliberately causes pain.

Suffering tests our faith in a loving God who claims to be our Father. Jesus himself shrank from personal suffering and so do we. It is human and natural to do so, but it is wrong to believe that suffering is good in itself or that God loves to see us suffer as a debt we owe for our sins. When we have explored every possible avenue of explanation we have to confess that why God allows suffering to happen is beyond our human comprehension. It is in the face of such suffering that we must hold firm to the belief that God is still our loving Father, even though in purely human terms what we witness in others and ourselves is a tragedy. The only value in suffering is the deepening of our faith and love of God the Father; without this, suffering is pointless. At healing services, when I come face to face with people in obvious pain and distress, my faith is tested and the concept of a loving God seems far removed from the situation before me. I would not even attempt to unravel the problem of pain, but I pray for a better understanding of it. We do not understand suffering in our own lives, our world or God's world. 'Who could ever know the mind of the Lord? Who could ever be his counsellor?' (Romans 11:34) We have to accept it in faith because this is all that is left to us.

People often come to our El Shaddai healing services because either they themselves or someone they love is suffering from a terminal disease. It is as if having tried everything else they turn to God for a miracle. They may think they are coming for healing but really they are desperately looking for magic. I feel very sorry for them because this is how they have been taught to see God. In such cases I believe that some healing always takes place if only we use love, patience and discernment. The very fact that they come to us to minister healing is a sign that they still have some sort of residual faith. In no way are they to be rejected because then it would appear that God, through us, was turning his back on them. The inner healing that can take place despite – and often because of – the distressing illness of someone we love is of inestimable value in allowing God's love and light to shine through the darkness. The ministry of healing in such cases is always extremely sensitive and reaches beyond the person who is ill to embrace the whole family and all those in any way connected with the person. It is often the terminal patient who is the healer of those around him or her. I bless and thank God for those who have come seeking his healing. In them I too find my healing, as I did with Frances.

Frances was a much-loved wife and mother who, in her early forties, was stricken with terminal cancer. I prayed with her many times for healing and the gift of inner peace. It is a gift I have rarely encountered in anyone other than those who are terminally ill. In the midst of the most excruciating pain she exuded a serenity which affected everyone who came in contact with her during her illness. She told me, 'I know that God loves me and I want to be physically healed so that I can look after my husband and children. So I pray every day for physical healing, I shall never give up hoping for that. But I believe, come what may, that God loves me and is very close to me. His peace is such that I can feel it deep inside. I have never experienced such peace before. It is as if I am alive for the first time in my life. He is my Father, but I keep on asking him what he is about. Anyway he knows best and I will leave it all to him.'

Frances died very peacefully. We prayed openly for her healing as a person, just as Jesus prayed for deliverance from his pain in Gethsemane. In her last few months on earth she showed no fear. Her faith reached a depth which less blessed people would envy and not understand. She is just one of hundreds whom the Father blessed in a way which was so wonderfully victorious over suffering and even death itself. God did not punish her with suffering. On the contrary, in her suffering he brought her deep inner peace. She looked on God as her loving Father and she never lost sight of that right to the end, when beyond death she began to live a new and fuller life with a God who never deserted her or those she loved. She faced dying with such faith and courage that she could say, 'Death is swallowed up in victory. Death, where is your victory? Death, where is your sting? (1 Corinthians 15:55)

If we do not have a personal love for God our Father, then we will never know him as Frances did; she really knew him as a father and a friend. It is sad that so many people believe that our approach to God should be something solemn and awesome so that, in worship, for example, it needs to be contained in liturgical ceremonies which often serve only to separate us from God. I remember one occasion when we were about to have a service of inner healing. All the people were happy, anticipating a celebration of God's healing presence among them. There was a buzz of expectancy in the church and a few children were innocently running up and down the aisle. An angry steward sternly warned the congregation that this was a house of prayer and worship and they were not to carry on as if they were in an ordinary house. He put a damper on everyone, though I soon remedied that! Later I discovered that he was a rigid disciplinarian, whose children, when they grew up, left the practice of their religion. I was not surprised; by the father's account, God was a kill-joy who did not approve of our parties, even though the gospel tells us that Jesus worked his first miracle by turning water into wine at the wedding feast in Cana. This, for the church steward, if he ever thought about it, was a one-off occasion, never to be repeated. Life was a hard grind and religion was only for the serious-minded. God's facial expression was a frown, never a smile.

This is not the God I know and see in people. God, for the church steward, had to be treated differently because he is not one of us. He is 'other' and so far away 'out there' that he is aloof from our way of life on earth. He doesn't really understand us when we say 'we cannot cope' and is so unbending in his justice that he judges us by his rule book and takes no account of us as persons. We have no excuse for our faults. He tells us that we have to 'get on with it' and make the best of a bad job when we know in our hearts that everything is falling apart in our lives and the lives of those whom we love and cherish. He certainly doesn't understand our silent tears because we feel so lost and don't know what to do or where to go for help. As far as we can decipher from the pattern of our lives, he sees suffering as something that it is inevitable because of our human condition. It is even something we deserve because of our wickedness. God is not really for us and is certainly not someone we can talk to or regard as a friend. The 'Our Father' was all right for Jesus, but not for us. God never answers our prayers because he is selective and likes only good, religious people and we are just not good enough. Because of our own overladen sense of guilt and unworthiness, we are convinced, and afraid, that God has deserted us and will not forgive us. He has written us off his list of those he loves because we are sinners and sinners we will remain.

Those who propagate this teaching are, in fact, fostering atheism. Religion that teaches fear and the threat of punishment destroys the notion of a loving God. This attitude to God is far more destructive of the human person than not to believe in God at all. At least if we believe that God does not exist then he cannot desert or punish us! A person brought up in a religion dominated by this type of servile fear of God chooses not to believe in God at all as the only way of finding some kind of inner peace so that he can live with himself.

This fear of a God who has abandoned us needs to be investigated and dispelled if we are to find true deep Christian peace. The God who is to be feared above all else is totally alien to the loving Father preached and lived out by Jesus. It is a false God. We need to reassure people tortured by such a caricature of God that the true God is their Father who will never desert them no matter what they have done. We cannot stop God, our Father, loving us: 'Does a woman forget her baby at the breast, or fail to cherish the son of her womb? Yet even if these forget, I will never forget you.' (Isaiah 49:15) We are all special to God. He has no favourites because he loves us all equally with his infinite, never-failing, never-ending love. His love is gratuitous. We can never merit it by our own unaided efforts because God has chosen us 'from the beginning to be saved by the sanctifying Spirit' (2 Thessalonians 2:13). 'Before the world was made, he chose us in Christ, . . . to live through love in his presence, determining that we should become his adopted sons through Jesus Christ' (Ephesians 1:4–5).

As Christians, we are loved by the Father who never leaves us as orphans, but for those who have been wrongly taught about the true meaning of healing then, in the final analysis, God cares only about our souls and not our bodies, so for them healing is completely spiritual. Suffering is seen as a sign of predestination for the specially chosen ones. The physical or emotional ailments which we suffer in this vale of tears might get us into heaven if we are fortunate enough. These are but some of the false ideas of God which still fill people's lives with an unwholesome fear, and from which, as Christians, we have a duty to free them. We have to encourage them to believe in a God who loves them as only a father could. This is the God whom Jesus loved and preached.

It is very difficult, and sometimes well-nigh impossible, for those who have never experienced the love of a human father to look on God as a loving father. They are denied their birthright not only as Christians but as human beings who should have been taught the healing power of love by their parents. For those who have experience only of possessive, cold, manipulative parents, towards whom they have bitter and hostile reactions, the word 'father' evokes such feelings of anger, frustration and even hatred that this spills over into their approach to God, whom they reject totally because of the damage which they have suffered at the hands of his human counterpart. Those who should have loved them have blighted their lives and, because of the deep inner damage they have suffered as a result of an unloved, unhappy childhood, they are ill-equipped to face the challenges of life. They often hate themselves because of their inner feelings of resentment towards their parents. Is it any wonder that Jesus told the people and his disciples, 'You must call no one on earth your father, since you have only one Father, and he is in heaven.' (Matthew 23:9)

Because we are all part of a large extended human family from the beginning to the end of time, then I tend to look on parents as our elder brothers and sisters. While I thank God for mine and what was passed from their lives into my attitude today to people and to God, I have every sympathy and compassion for those who are not so blessed. They are 'orphans' living in what should be a loving family situation. They are the handicapped children of our time who need protective love and com-passion. They are eagles who as eaglets have never been taught how to fly. Such a person is Mary and this is her story, as she told it to me.

'My parents never told me they loved me. They never hugged me or showed me any real affection. I envied the other children at school when I saw how their mothers were so open and warm towards them. I felt so out of it. My mother always made sure that I was clean and tidy, but I wanted more than the outward appearances. I wanted to be loved and told that I was special. I found out later on that my mother was herself the child of a lifeless, loveless marriage. My father's background was exactly the same. It is only now many years after their death that I feel sorry for them. They never knew what love was and were afraid and unable to show it to each other, so how could they show it to me? Largely because of their attitude and the atmosphere in the home, I became drawn in on myself and was unable to make friends. I respected my parents and did everything they asked of me to win their approval, but there was a deadness inside. Now I know that I ached for them to tell me how they felt towards me. Were they glad I was their daughter or did I just happen because they were married? I don't know and I never shall because they both died without telling me.

'I thought I was the only one who felt like this until I came to an El Shaddai healing service. A woman gave a testimony of how she was treated as a child and how she felt. It was an exact replica of my situation. She told the congregation how she had not only to forgive her parents but also to feel genuinely sorry for them because they too were victims of loveless marriages. She explained how difficult it was to free herself from the entangled web of hurtful memories of her childhood. After that service God gave me the grace to forgive my parents and the courage to change my life-style. Fortunately I was able to share my background with my husband and young children. They are helping me, and I hope I am helping them, to have a warm loving family atmosphere. My children give me more love than I deserve, but I need it as a parched land needs water. I try not to be selfish or manipulative. It is not easy to love as a parent. Now I am beginning to understand in a very small way why Jesus called God his Father. It is the only title he should be known by because he loves us as we yearn to be loved. My whole life is changed and now, at the age of forty-two, I am beginning to grow with my family day by day. My Christian faith is showing me how to love as a parent should.'

Mary's testimony had a happy ending, but it is not always so. She was fortunate in that she was able to share her history with her family, but there are many 'family victims' who are unable to talk about the things that really hurt them in their childhood. They are so crippled that they are like a person in a cage in which they feel isolated and from which they are unable to break free. The increasing breakdown in family life and the unhappiness it causes in children makes us more sensitive to the needs of young people, who are tomorrow's parents. Mary and others like her need a deep healing of memories which can only take place over a long period of time. I shall deal with this and with the problems faced by children sexually abused by their parents in later chapters of this book.

Once we get our relationship right with God – and we can only do this by recognising and acknowledging him as our Father who wants what is best for us and never stops loving us – then our lives will change. This love of God as our Father will unblock all the bitterness, anger and resentment which we feel towards others because of their ill-treatment of us. We will love ourselves in a new way because we will learn to know and love ourselves as we are in God's eyes. His love is the yardstick of our love of ourselves. We are his children and he wants us whole and healthy. Uncontrolled fear will have no part in our lives once we dare to call God our Father. This is the source of our healing from fear: 'Love will come to perfection in us when we can face the day of Judgement without fear . . . In love there can be no fear, but fear is driven out by perfect love: because to fear is to expect punishment' (1 John 4:17–18).

5

Afraid to Pray for Healing

We are afraid to pray for healing because we don't know how. We have never been trained or encouraged to do it. Yet this form of prayer was very much part of Jesus' own prayer life. When he prayed for healing for others he always called with confidence on his Father (for example, John 11:41–42) to answer his plea on behalf of those who came to him seeking curing and healing. There are many reasons why we do not see prayers for healing as set into our Christian prayer life. It may be because of our false, exaggerated view of the value of suffering or because of our failure to look on God as a Father who wants our wholeness and health. We tend to regard him as someone who sends us suffering because it is good for us. This concentration on our own sinfulness and unworthiness rather than God's fatherly love for us has deprived our Christian lives of the nourishment which healing prayer brings. It is a rich field which has long been left fallow because it has not been put to the plough. Once we till it, then the harvest will yield a hundredfold and we will begin to see this form of prayer as a new fulfilling way of living the Christian life. We will be amazed at how we ever survived without it. It will control fear and bring us deep inner peace in a way which nothing else ever could.

People are for ever asking me to advise them as to how they should pray, especially for healing. It was the same in the time of Christ. His disciples asked him, 'Lord, teach us to pray' (Luke 11:1). His answer was simple: he gave them the Lord's Prayer. Yet this prayer is not the same in Matthew's Gospel (6:9–13) as it is in Luke's version. Though they are both *essentially* the same and contain the main points of Our Lord's prayer and teaching, nevertheless they are not word-for-word replicas. Why? Because prayer is basically *personal.* We pray best when we use our own words in our own way. The trouble with many of us is not only that we tend to see prayer in set formal structures, but also that we are *impersonal* in our prayer.

In the early days of El Shaddai, I was afraid of being too personal in my prayers for healing because it had been drilled into me that the important thing was to say prayers without letting anything of myself creep into them. I prayed and was not changed, whereas every prayer should heal and change us. Why did this happen? I think it was because I believed that prayers, like the sacraments, had an intrinsic effectiveness of their own, irrespective of my personal input. In fact, I believed they were better when I said them in an attitude in which, in my mind and heart, I thought little or nothing of myself or my own worth. This was called 'humility'. I was praying to 'someone out there', a 'power' who would decide whether or not he would condescend to listen and in his goodness answer me. I did not talk to God as my friend and Father, as Jesus did when he prayed. Now I look on prayer as a conversation, in which I know from experience as well as faith that God does listen. It is this type of prayer that changes our lives and us as persons. It heals us of all the pains and hurts of the past as well as controlling our fears about the future. 'Prayers' don't change us, but 'prayer' does. One is words, the other is a dialogue between friends with whom we share our deepest thoughts, our dreams and our fears.

No one can really teach us how to pray in a completely identical way to the manner in which they themselves pray. You and I pray differently! But if we both pray in the Spirit, then your prayer touches my mind and heart and encourages me to pray in a *similar* way. It is God in both of us who is praying. We are like an orchestra playing the same melody but with different instruments.

The only way to learn to pray is to pray and the only way to pray well is to pray often. All true prayer comes from God's spirit within us. This is what gives our words meaning and authenticity. We are not parrots mouthing noises meant to be prayer. We speak from the heart, from the depths within us. In his preface to the Lord's Prayer, Jesus said: 'In your prayers do not babble as the pagans do, for they think that by using many words they will make themselves heard. Do not be like them; your Father knows what you need before you ask him. So you should pray *like* this . . .' (Matthew 6:7–9). Even with his own special prayer, Jesus said we were to pray *like* it. We were not to copy it exactly as he said it, as long as what we said contained the main points of what the prayer was all about. His prayer touches our hearts and so in Spirit we are united with him as we say the 'Our Father'. If we said this prayer really well, just once, it would change our lives. It is quality, not quantity, that matters.

Prayer for Jesus, as for every Christian, is something which flowed from his life of faith and love. He was a God-the-Father-orientated person. Prayer is a love affair between two people – God the Father and myself. When I am ill and not at peace within myself, for whatever reason, then he expects me to talk with him about it. Isn't this what friends are for? It means that, like Jesus, I am aware that the most important force in my life is God the Father's love for me. He sees each one of us as unique. This is how we need to see ourselves when we pray – not as we see ourselves, but as God our Father sees us. Then, and only then, will we begin to understand with whom and to whom we are praying. We will really begin to pray in the Spirit and become more healed, more whole as people. We know that someone who loves us is listening to us and answering all our needs. When we listen to him, he will explain better than we can what our needs really are.

I know, from my own experience, that for years I said prayers, but I did not pray as deeply as I do now that I have discovered that God the Father loves me. He is my best friend, and I try to share everything with him – the ups and downs, the good times and the bad, the small as well as the big things. It has completely changed my life. God is not only my father; he is your father too. This is the gospel, the good news that Jesus brings to all who believe in him. None of us is an orphan as long as we believe in God. God is a better father than the best father who ever lived. This is what Jesus taught as essential to his gospel. He was forever talking of his Father's love for us. This is the message that, as Christians, we should pass on to one another. 'Is there a man among you who would hand his son a stone when he asked for bread? Or would hand him a snake when he asked for a fish? If you, then, who are evil, know how to give your children what is good, how much more will your Father in heaven give good things to those who ask him!' (Matthew 7:9–11)

It is hard to believe fully in God the Father's unique love for us. In fact it will take us a lifetime to grow in our understanding of it and even then our grasp of what it means will be only partial. We know we don't deserve it, but if God loves us then there is nothing we can do about it. We cannot change him, but we can allow him to change us. Prayer for healing will do just that. This is why Jesus, who understood his Father in a unique way, encouraged us to pray for healing. He knew that this is what his Father wants us to do. In his own suffering, Jesus prayed to be free of it, so why shouldn't we? God is not immune to our pain and all the various emotional, physical or spiritual handicaps which prevent us from growing as persons. It is to his glory that we should be healed. This is why in El Shaddai, in our everyday healing, we give glory to God, our loving, caring Father. When I pray for healing for myself, I know that God is loving me in a much more powerful way than I could ever begin to love or heal myself. My love for myself is limited and selfish, but there are no boundaries, no conditions, in God's love for me, except to accept it and remain close to him. He will do the rest. The gospel of Jesus constantly reminds us that all he said and did during his lifetime on earth was nothing other than to show his Father's love for you and me. 'The words I say to you I do not speak as from myself: it is the Father, living in me, who is doing this work.' (John 14:10) God answers our prayer for healing by his actions in our life. Jesus is God the Father with a human face. All healing, like all prayer, flows from our awareness and acceptance of God the Father's love for us. He alone heals us, and meets all our needs through his son Jesus Christ. Fear, which wants to control us, tells us that there is no point in praying because God just cannot be bothered with all our petty little requests; he is far too busy in his world to be concerned with ours.

The gospel of Jesus reminds us that God knows our needs better than we know them ourselves. For years I know that I prayed for all the things that I wanted. I told God what was good for me! I never asked him what he thought. Jesus has great sympathy with our selfish approach. The night before he died, because he was fully human, he did not want to suffer and so he prayed, 'Father, if it is possible, let this cup [of suffering] pass me by. Nevertheless, let it be as you, not I, would have it.' (Matthew 26:39)

Prayer makes us aware of our real *needs* rather than our *wants*. In prayer we seek to discover what is God's will for us because he wants, and is able, to give us what is best for us. All prayer and healing is rooted in our trust that God our Father will provide for all our needs. The more we pray, and the deeper our prayers, the more we realise that God has a plan for our lives once we identify our lives with his. We will never cease to be amazed how wonderfully he looks after us. That is why all prayer should begin, and end, in praise. I find in reading, and trying to live out the gospel, that once I trust God with my life then all will come right.

I find in the ministry of healing that many people are unable to distinguish between their needs and their wants. I may want to minister healing to a young person with multiple sclerosis, and he may want it himself, but if neither of us tries to discover what is God's will, we will have missed out on the whole meaning of prayer, healing and life. Prayer takes me into the mystery of God and I would rather leave things to him than put myself in sole control of what happens to me or to those I love. If I can live just one day at a time in his love and presence, then I shall be doing exactly what Jesus did and what he asks of us. God my Father will look after tomorrow just as well as he looked after today.

As Christians we want to do God's will, yet we don't seem to know where to start. We can be pretty certain that we will not have a blinding revelation such as Saul had on the road to Damascus. I am suspicious of people who claim to receive special miraculous daily messages from God telling them what to do. When they say that they have a message from God for me, I weigh up what they say in the light of what kind of person they are. If they really have a message, then God will give me the grace to listen and respond. But as a rule, I prefer to wait until God will show me in his own good time which road he wants me to take. I have enough difficulty in deciphering his message for me without pretending to have messages for anyone else! Some people have messages for others at the drop of a hat. *Beware of false prophets*! They seem to know more than Jesus and Our Lady did in their lifetime about God's will for them.

Jesus acknowledged that to discover God's will for him was a search that would last until the day he died. He never claimed to know God the Father's will for him before the actual event. After prayer, he would have to make a decision on what he should do. In the Garden of Gethsemane his human response to the suffering he was about to undergo was to escape from it, but it was not to be. There was no escaping his Father's will. The same Jesus who gave us, in his prayer to the Father, the words 'Thy will be done on earth as it is in heaven' had now to put them into effect. His death was God's will for him, but so was the resurrection. God's will for Jesus was ultimately for his life, not his death. Jesus told the two disciples on the road to Emmaus, 'Was it not ordained that the Christ should suffer and so enter into his glory?' (Luke 24:26).

Mary, his mother, did not fully understand the consequences behind the message of the angel, ' "Mary do not be afraid; you have won God's favour. Listen! You are to conceive and bear a son, and you must name him Jesus." . . . Mary said to the angel, "But how can this come about, since I am a virgin?" "The Holy Spirit will come upon you" the angel answered, "and the power of the Most High will cover you with its shadow. And so the child will be holy and will be called Son of God." ' (Luke 1:31–35) God's will for Mary, as for Jesus, is for life. We too have to seek and search for God's will for us. God wants us to live fully each moment of every day, and we have to discover this day by day. It is a gradual process because the mystery of God's will for us is the mystery of self. It is an attempt to discover who we are and what our lives are all about.

John is a typical example of the hundreds who write to us or whom we meet at healing services. 'I have never looked on God as someone who loved me. For me, he was a stern judge who would stick by the letter of the law, and punish me for all the wrong things I did in my life. I certainly did not trust him. I didn't love him. I feared him. He was so demanding that I lived in absolute dread of when I would meet him after I died. If I was lucky I might make it to heaven, and then only after a long time in purgatory. My life was dominated by fear and sin, not love and happiness. I lived in an atmosphere of fear fuelled by religion which told me to behave myself. I went to church as a payment against the debt of my sins. Then I came to one of the El Shaddai healing services. I heard you telling me, as if I was the only person in the crowded church, that God loved me and wanted what was best for me. You said I had to trust him with my life. Well, I'm trying to do just that, but it is an up-and-down business. When I fail I keep on remembering that God loves me, and this is my lifeline. It keeps me from drowning. But somewhere deep down inside me I have found the secret of life. God's love heals, and I need a lot of healing. I now know that I have to work out the direction of my life with God and no one can do it for me. But I ask you please to remember me in your prayers that I shall continue to trust God with my life.'

Why God acts the way he does is beyond our limited vision of life to comprehend. 'How rich are the depths of God' says St Paul, 'how deep his wisdom and knowledge – and how impossible to penetrate his motives or understand his methods! Who could ever know the mind of the Lord? Who could ever be his counsellor?' (Romans 11:33–34) By all means we should question him when things come our way which disturb our inner peace. I'm always asking God 'Why?'. 'Why, Lord, is this young mother of four children, all under six years, dying of cancer? Why did young Jim commit suicide when he had so much to live for? Why did the lovely young couple whom I married find it impossible to continue living with each other?' I have as many 'Whys' as I have people to minister to at every healing service. But in the final analysis I have to leave it to him:

> In the blest hereafter, I shall know
> Why in His wisdom, He hath led me so.

It is in some ways a slight on God if we accept suffering without question. It seems as if we believe that God wants to punish us, or is unwilling or unable to help us. I need to reconcile his fatherhood and his power to heal, so I question him, and when I do I also give him time to answer me. In prayer he calms our troubled minds and hearts. In some mysterious way, in the midst of the storm, God is healing me even when I see everything around me falling to pieces. 'Since God did not spare his own Son, but gave him up to benefit us all, we may be certain, after such a gift, that he will not refuse anything he can give.' (Romans 8:32)

An inspiration to me in my limited understanding of God's purpose for me, especially when things seem to go wrong, has been the prayer of Cardinal Newman:

> I will trust God. Whatever, wherever I am, I can
>   never be thrown away.
> If I am in sickness, my sickness may serve him;
> In perplexity, my perplexity may serve him.
> He does nothing in vain. He knows what he is about.
> He may take away my friends. He may throw me
>   among strangers.
> He may make me feel desolate, make my spirits sink,
> Hide my future from me, still he knows what he
>   is about.

We need to trust God because left to ourselves we would fail. Sin has invaded the whole fabric of our lives. It has weakened us to the extent that even in our inmost self we are divided, in conflict. 'I cannot understand my own behaviour. I fail to carry out the things I want to do, and I find myself doing the very things I hate . . . though the will to do what is good is in me, the performance is not, with the result that instead of doing the good things I want to do, I carry out the sinful things I do not want.' (Romans 7:15, 18) Our sinfulness clouds our vision of life and give us a distorted picture of who we are. We get ourselves out of focus and we don't know what to pray for or when or whether to pray at all. Maybe we are never going to discover what is God's will for us, so why begin the search?

George helps to illustrate the point I am trying to make. For years he had a very poor self-image. 'I didn't think much of myself,' he wrote. 'I thought the world was a pretty rotten place. I had no goals in my life except to have as good a time as possible. I left home to take up a dull job. I led the usual aimless life. Then, through a friend, I went along to a Pentecostal group where everyone seemed to be on a high. They seemed to see God in everything, and it was not long before I too became one of them. I was a born-again Christian! I stayed with this group for about a year but in my heart of hearts I felt I was playing a game of make-believe. For me at least it did not bring me into contact with reality. So I left, despite the pressures on me to stay. I was in a real mess because now I felt I had rejected religion. Seven years ago I came with my friends to a Catholic healing service. I treated the whole affair with suspicion, but before the service was over I knew that this approach to life and to God was completely right for me. It was balanced. It didn't tell me I was saved, nor was I going to spend eternity in hell's fire. Over the past seven years my life has had a purpose, and I know that God is my Father who loves me. It is the awareness of this love which has changed my life.'

George is more attuned to God's will for him because he knows that God's love overcomes his own sinfulness. He knows that he cannot make it alone. When he allowed God to enter his life, he began to appreciate that he could change and find a true meaning to life. If we want to understand God's will for us then we will set his love for us against our own inner weakness. The scales will be finely balanced. We will begin to have a true appreciation of who we are and what is the next step on the road to a true discovery of God's will for us and for our healing.

If we want to discover God's will then we must be patient with ourselves. He wants us to live in peace, not only with him, but also with ourselves. Worry or anxiety on our part is not his plan for us. We are to possess our souls in peace. Above all we are not to feel guilty about the past. God has taken away our guilt by the love and suffering of his own son. Those who feel irrationally guilty about the past are dimming the light of God's love in the present moment. When the time comes for us to act in a certain way, God's Spirit will be there counselling and encouraging us. Our service for him will be in perfect freedom because we do it in the context of love. We must not be afraid. When we have done our best we have to leave the end result to God. We know in faith that he loves us as our Father, and we trust him in hope that what we do is according to his will. 'We know that by turning everything to their good, God co-operates with all those who love him' (Romans 8:28). I have found that the only way to true peace of mind and heart is to live life as best I can. God knows that in my own small way I love him. This is the secret of life and of inner peace.

I have written so far about how we should talk to God about our needs, but prayer means listening as well as talking. Recently, when I was on a train to London, two people sitting opposite to me never stopped talking, supposedly to each other. But neither listened to the other, and listening is a sign of love and respect for the other person. As a young priest I was preoccupied with 'getting my prayers in'. I said a lot of prayers, but I don't think I prayed a lot. My prayers in some vague way added to the noise in my life. However much I increased their quantity, they did not make me a peace-filled person. Many people complain to me that God never listens to their prayers. Of course he does, but if they don't listen to him then he won't be able to get a word in edgeways! We live in a world of noise without communication. We will never get anywhere in prayer if we treat our conversation with God in the same way.

As people grow in love they do not feel the need for words. As I have grown older I have lost my fear of what God might ask of me. Previously I was afraid of silence lest he would talk to me about the contradictions in my life-style. He is not like that at all. He will change us gently, but only if we genuinely want to be changed. If not, he will let us get on with our prayers until we realise how fruitless they are. We will either give up prayers, or we will listen to him. When we listen, then he can begin to heal us.

I think that discernment is indispensable to healing. Until we discern what is God's will for an individual who comes to our ministry of healing then it is pointless saying prayers over, or for, them. They are meaningless words and actions. We need to discern what is God's will for us too before we embark on praying for others. We will only do this if we listen with our hearts as well as our minds to God. Although speech is a necessary means of communication, nevertheless, there is a whole new world of self-discovery which opens up before us where silence is the only true means of communication. This is why I speak few words when I minister to people during healing services. What God says to them, and to me, is much more important than what we say to him. I do not relate to people in the ministry of healing who, as a rule, spend lots of time and words with people instead of *being* for a short while to them, and then leaving them to God. He is closer to them than we could ever hope to be.

The silence of prayer brings us deep inner peace. Jennie, a young mother of four children, found such peace some years ago when she gave herself and her whole family to God. From that moment all her worries ceased, and the cancer which was ravaging her body was brought under control. Her life is completely changed.

She knows that God is her father who never refuses to give her his peace. Prayer brings us into the eye of the storm in our lives where everything is calm and still. 'Be still and know that I am God' is a promise to us all who look on God as our loving Father. Peace is Christ's gift to us. In prayer we know that nothing is more precious or more healing. It is for this reason that we call ourselves at El Shaddai 'A Christian Movement for *Inner* Healing'.

In times of stress when things are not going our way, then of course we worry. We are anxious. Jesus knows that. He saw it in the crowds who followed him, and in the disciples who, in the midst of a storm on a lake, accused him of not caring because he had his head on a cushion, asleep! When we pray in times of hardship and suffering and leave the end result to God, then peace will flood our soul. We will rise up from prayer knowing that we are not afraid of any storm in life which we have to face. Jesus has calmed storms in our lives before and, aware that he is with us, we are at peace within ourselves because we know that all will be well.

Whenever I go into a packed church where hundreds of people are expecting God to heal them, I do not worry because I am quite certain that he will give his peace to all who are open to his Spirit. We have to be on our guard, however, against those events and people which disrupt and destroy our peace, even in the setting of a healing service in church. It is not a performance, a 'show'. It is a gentle waiting on God to heal us. We do not have to strive or reach out for this inner peace: it will come to us when we rest in God's Spirit and will strengthen us with a power which fills us with light and life.

Prayer in the Spirit makes us confident, *not arrogant*, that through God's love for us we are special people. 'Think of the love that the Father has lavished on us, by letting us be called God's children; and that is what we are' (1 John 3:1). In prayer I know that God loves me and that he wants me to be whole and happy. He also wants me to be healed, to see that my life has a unique purpose, and to realise that there will never be another me! One of the main results of inner healing is to make us realise that we need to love ourselves because God is our Father who loves us first. If I don't love myself I can't love anyone. This is why, quietly confident of who we are, we are able to pray for others, that they may experience his healing gift of the awareness of God's love for them. I find an echo of this in St John's words, 'We are quite confident that if we ask him for anything, and it is in accordance with his will, he will hear us; and, knowing that whatever we may ask, he hears us, we know that we have *already* been granted what we asked of him.' (1 John 5:14–15) We know that what we have prayed for, according to our loving Father's will, is already granted even though we may not recognise it immediately. Our prayer, therefore, for healing should always end in thanksgiving. The victory is ours.

While Christians are special people, nevertheless there is a false confidence in some who minister in healing which smacks of elitism as if they are special people in such a way as to set them apart and above others. This is alien to the gospel, and to the thinking of our El Shaddai movement. God has no favourites. In prayer we are all equal. Whenever I minister in healing I consider myself to be privileged that I am used as a channel, however small, of God the Father's love for his people. The people to whom I minister are probably closer to God than I am and through the witness of their faith and love they minister healing to me.

I never hedge my bets in my prayers for healing for others. God is a 'yes' and a 'no' person when it comes to listening to him. If he wants us to do something then we just do it. It is as simple as that. We have to be open to him in faith and pray to empty ourselves of self-seeking. I always start by praying for inner peace for the person to whom I feel called to minister. Then if the Lord wants me to do more I just pray for that intention absolutely and unconditionally. Jesus commanded the winds and waves to die down, just as he ordered sickness out of people who cried out to him to have pity on them. If we wish to be close to God, he will show us how to pray. Unfortunately, many people ask for things beyond the measure of their prayer. This brings the ministry of healing into disrepute by creating false and unfounded hope when we ask for something out of our emotional situation rather than based on prayer. Confidence in prayer and discernment will grow, but the only real teacher is the Holy Spirit. He will show us what to pray for and when he does we will ask with confidence and complete trust.

Praying for healing should be as normal to us as the air we breathe. It is part and parcel of our everyday life. We do not need to look for very exact, high-sounding phrases and words in order to express what is in our hearts. Prayer is not an intelligence test. The simpler and shorter the prayer the better. While I accept the beauty of many set forms of prayer, nevertheless, the words that just come 'tumbling out' are often much more authentic. I remember an open-air Mass for handicapped children at which, one by one, they read out bidding prayers which had obviously been carefully written out for them before-hand by their parents. One boy of about twelve was about to read out his petition when a gust of wind blew it out of his hands. As he watched it disappear into the sky, he lifted his hands in dismay and said, 'Jesus, I am sorry, but I do love you.' He said it all. It is in moments of great joy or sadness that the words come most naturally to our lips because they are already in our heart. My favourite prayer in *The Treasury of the Holy Spirit* concerns judgement time. It was written by Paul Claudel and says everything to my spirit.

> Have pity upon every man, Lord, in that hour when he has finished his task and stands before thee like a child, whose hands are being examined.

We need to be ourselves when we pray for healing. I find it hard to accept artificiality. It sounds so counterfeit. If only our prayers at church were more ordinary, and down to earth, then people would really believe that we were talking to a God whom we believe listens to us. We should be able to slip from ordinary conversation into prayer without any change of voice or the choice of words we normally use. After all, God is with us as our friend.

I used to feel slightly embarrassed when people asked me to pray for them and for those they loved. I promised I would and did so later, but I never stopped there and then to pray with them. It seemed as if they thought that, as a priest, I was better than they were. I now realise it is a most natural thing in the world for us to pray for each other. The tragedy is, as I said earlier, that because of our training we tend to be formal and impersonal in our prayers. Perhaps it is because of our culture that we are reluctant to reveal our inmost thoughts and feelings to one another. We are also afraid to pray out loud in spontaneous prayer in the presence of others. Before I became fully involved in the healing ministry I thought that prayer was too personal a thing for me to do with someone listening to me. Now praying *with* people is so very much part of my life that I could hardly visualise it as being otherwise. It has been a blessing and a healing for me.

We need to be set free from this fear of praying openly with one another which blunts our Christian life. When we pray with others *we can sense the love of Christ in our midst.* 'I tell you solemnly once again, if two of you on earth agree to ask anything at all, it will be granted to you by my Father in heaven. For where two or three meet in my name, I shall be there with them.' (Matthew 18:19–20) This is why practically all of my healing ministry in prayer is exercised with El Shaddai teams. They help me to pray with and for others. When people pray at a healing service for each other then I am much more aware of God's power among them. The prayer of a loving family always heals. In my youth the family rosary was part of my life and growing-up. Today it seems a shame that parents don't pray with their children and bless them by touching them on the head. If we pray with others they will not feel so alone.

It should be obvious to every Christian that we are all called to heal each other. We do this by prayer. Unfortunately we have lost sight of this privilege by restricting the ministry of healing prayer to priests and nuns. As Christians we are called to pray for each other's healing. This is why I always ask the team to pray for me before I begin any ministry in a church service for inner healing. All of you who read this book are invited to pray with us every evening at El Shaddai. We are all members of the Christian family. When we pray for others we show our love for God our Father in our care and concern for other people. This is the most effective form of healing prayer. Our prayer of healing for others also heals ourselves. The person who thinks he is a minister of healing but sees no need for healing in or for himself is far removed from the gospel of Christ. Our love for others, however deep, is but a shadow of God's love for us all. A prayer for healing is quite simply a 'love prayer'. We can never have enough love, enough healing.

Only God's love can heal. He will use our prayers to heal those for whom we pray in a way far more powerful than we can ask or imagine. Our love for those in need of healing helps both us and them to make contact with God's love. We know we cannot fulfil the deep longing of their hearts, but we join with them in their prayer for healing so that they are no longer alone. Christ who is with us when we pray, takes our healing prayer to the Father on our behalf. This is why in faith we believe that our prayers for healing will be answered because it is Christ's prayer for us and for those we love which heals.

There will be times in all our lives when we suffer emotionally, physically and spiritually. Suffering disturbs our inner peace. It is easy to pray when suffering is something 'out there', affecting other people, but when it enters our own lives we remain shocked and numb. I always find it difficult to pray in times of my own personal suffering, and so I need the prayers and strength of others. It is through others that I am encouraged to turn my suffering from something *destructive* of my peace into a *creative* deep sense of inner peace which no one can take from me. It is when we are suffering that we need someone with whom we can share the sorrow which eats into the depth of our being. Jesus took Peter, James and John into the Garden of Gethsemane so that they would be with him as he suffered. The example of Jesus is there for us in healing prayer. We need to share our suffering with others who will help us to bear the burden. We also need to share our joy and love for each other.

In compassion we share with Christ in the pain of our wounded brother and sister. In them we see not only the wounded person, but our own wounded selves. Jesus reminds us that in times of suffering we grow in peace and a closer following of him. In the ministry of healing we encourage people to look on the wounded Christ and understand in faith that by his wounds we are healed. All ministers of healing suffer with the wounded people for whom they pray. This is compassion – suffering with another – and the linking of our pain with that of Jesus himself. What is sad is that there are so few who share *within* themselves in Christian healing prayer the sufferings of others. Many, if not most, people suffer alone. In the ministry of healing we identify ourselves with Christ in the pain of others. We are one with them as they walk through the valley of darkness. Christ encourages all who suffer to believe that there is light at the end of the tunnel. He shares within himself the pain of others. He invites us in the ministry of healing to do the same. It is a painful road, which includes the cross, but takes us beyond it into a new world of healing peace lit up by the resurrection. In healing we begin to discover what life, suffering and prayer are all about. We may be wounded in our minds and bodies but we know that as Christians we share in Christ's victory over all kinds of suffering, even death itself. There are others more wounded than we are. This is why we need to overcome our fear of praying for the healing of all our wounded brothers and sisters. In them, as in Christ, we are healed.

We are not being proud or arrogant or pretending to be holier-than-thou when we pray for another person's healing. We are doing exactly what every ordinary Christian should do. The devil would have us believe that we are not holy enough to have our prayers heard on our own behalf, let alone when they are offered for others. I am only too well aware that some people put on an act when they pray, but if we sincerely believe that in spite of our faults Jesus *needs* us to pray through him so that he can take our petitions to the Father, then we will pray and it will become easier with practice. 'I tell you most solemnly,' said Jesus, 'anything you ask for from the Father he will grant in my name.' (John 16:23)

Unfortunately many church-going people and even families do not pray openly for and with each other because they are afraid of being different. The Charismatic Renewal movement has done a great deal to heal us of this inhibition which has for so long denied many of us the privilege of praying as Christ really wanted his followers to do. It is true that 'we are only the earthenware jars that hold this treasure, to make it clear that such an overwhelming power [in prayer] comes from God and not from us' (2 Corinthians 4:7). But it is a power the devil does not want us to have, and that is why he tries to overwhelm us with our own unworthiness. We may be only earthenware jars, but the healing ointment they contain will fill God's house with its fragrance. God loves us and the person we are praying for more than we do. He loves us enough, however bad we may seem to ourselves, to answer our prayers. The force which heals is God's love for his children. In praying for others we will be healed ourselves, knowing that we are part of the Christian family which wants everyone to be healed, whole and healthy. Even though we are wounded ourselves, we have the strength and confidence to pray for the healing of others. 'Any one of you who is ill should send for the elders of the church and they must anoint the sick person with oil in the name of the Lord and pray over him. The prayer of faith will save the sick person and the Lord will raise him up again' (James 5:14–15).

6

Afraid of Change

Life means change. Where there is no change there is no life. Life can never remain static. Not all change, however, is good for our growth as persons. Things can happen which so affect us that we are damaged and our quality of life is adversely affected. We need, therefore, to *discern* which changes are for our good and which are not. As far as possible, we have to choose to accept those changes which will benefit us and make us more alive, more human. *There is no change which cannot be used to help us to grow as persons.* Jesus used his crucifixion to heal our world because he gave the pains which he would suffer in his passion to his loving Father. 'Out of evil cometh good.' Our growth as persons is in proportion to our openness to, and discernment of, change. We will never be able to discern change correctly if we refuse to be open to its challenge so that we can face it without bigotry or prejudice. A closed mind and heart which are opposed to all change stunt the individual's personal growth. It kills him within because he has withdrawn himself from life.

If we really want to become more alive as persons – in other words, to grow up and mature – we must be prepared to change our childish attitudes and ways. We were meant to live as adults in an adult world. Just as we get older with the passage of time, we should also become more mature, more experienced, responsible and understanding. Life comes to us moment by moment because we live in time and time always marches on. Things of today are not the same as yesterday. They never were and never could be. At every moment of our lives we are changing, whether we like it or not. From birth to death we live by a constant succession of changes. We have to learn to live with all the changes in our lives and use them as creatively as possible. If we oppose change in any area of our lives which would help us to grow as persons, then we die in that area of our personality, whether it be physical, emotional or spiritual. We become less a person than we would have been if we had accepted change. Healing is all about learning how to deal with the events in our lives so that we are able and encouraged to grow as persons.

Change is our life-giving oxygen by which as persons we breathe and grow, and yet there is something in all of us which shrinks from change, especially changing ourselves and our attitudes. This really threatens us. Because time never stands still it ages us relentlessly and, like King Canute, we cannot turn back the tide. We know that our bodies age because we can feel it, yet we are so often afraid of growing old. If we face up to it, then we know we cannot remain as young and physically vital as children forever. We have to grow up too in our emotions and attitudes to life, and this is much more difficult. As Christians, we have to grow in our attitude to God and mature in our relationship with him. As we grow in our understanding of ourselves and others, we also grow in our relationship with God. We see him more clearly through people and events which help to form us into the kind of person we become.

Throughout his life 'Jesus grew in wisdom and stature' (Luke 2:52). He was open to change and he is an example to us of how we should live in a changing world. Change fills us with fear the more we fail to adapt to it. Unless we control it, then it builds up a tension within us which overloads like electricity and eventually fuses and destroys our lives. As I said earlier, if we really want to become more fully alive we need change, movement, much as a river needs the inflow of fresh-water from streams to keep it moving because otherwise it stagnates. Healing unblocks the areas opposed to change which prevent us from living more fully and more peacefully. Healing helps us to integrate all the changes, whatever they may be, into our lives at every level so that we grow through them. Change is the essence of life, bringing us the hope and joy of challenge and discovery. It gives us a thrill, a sense of adventure, a feeling that it is good to be alive. There can be no Christian healing without it because basically it means changing ourselves and allowing ourselves to lead the new life in Christ. Conversion to Christ radically changes our lives so that we become new persons, 'and for anyone who is in Christ there is a new creation. The old creation has gone and now the new one is here. It is all God's work' (2 Corinthians 5:17). Cardinal Newman wrote that 'to live is to change and to be perfect is to have changed often'. Every time we receive Christian healing, we are changed as persons. Change through healing involves our growth so that we become more fully human, fully alive, fully Christian. It is a renewal of life and it is like being born again. Christians who are obsessively afraid of change are automatically afraid of life: they want to stay where they are and this is a hopeless situation and attitude. The Christian life is all about dealing with change and to be opposed completely to it is to turn our backs on the gospel message preached and lived by Jesus.

All through our lives we are in constant, even daily, need of healing. Why? So that we may be ready in joy and hope to grow through all the changes and challenges which come our way in our pilgrimage of life. If we want to become more like the person God our Father wants us to be then we must be free from all those fears which would burden us and prevent us from crossing new frontiers in our lives. Faith fills us with expectancy, fear with foreboding. People of faith live in today's world, sensitive to the Spirit calling for change in us because our world is changing and needs our Christian witness of freedom, joy and hope. Yesterday's people constantly talk of the good old days. They cannot or will not read the signs of the times in case this would disturb their secure lives. 'The Pharisees and Sadducees came, and to test Jesus, asked if he would show them a sign from heaven. He replied, 'In the evening you say, "It will be fine; there is a red sky," and in the morning, "Stormy weather today; the sky is red and overcast". You know how to read the face of the sky, but you cannot read the signs of the times.' (Matthew 16:1–3) For those completely opposed to change, like the Pharisees, nothing is allowed to rock their boat. They batten down the hatches and ride out the storm when a gale blows up. Their destination is nowhere because they have turned their craft into a houseboat in which they live, rather than a vessel in which they sail into uncharted waters. Because they could not read the signs of the times, with their consequent changes, the Pharisees missed out on the Messiah. We can be today's Pharisees if our attitude to change is as unyielding as theirs.

People who are fearful of change cannot adapt to changing situations in their lives. They have no real vision of joy or hope because they have lost the spirit of adventure. Change in any form, whether it be emotional, physical or spiritual, threatens them and so the glorification of the *status quo* is their ultimate idea of happiness. They are pessimists who can envisage no change for the better. Basically they are not Christians because they are blind to the gospel message of hope and change. Long ago they have ceased to dream dreams or to see visions. They are the living dead who divest religion of faith and have dug for themselves a routine which is a rut deeper than a grave. Jesus shared with his followers his dreams of a world in love with his Father. We dream our dreams too of a Christian people living with life in today's world and responding to the Holy Spirit's invitation to us to take a risk, to be pilgrims in search of a new Jerusalem which will unfold before our eyes over the next mountain-top. Dreamers may be few, but they change our world and Church because they are prepared to pay the price for their dreams. They are eagles who fly alone and not in groups. Once we allow ourselves to be open to change, then we are divested of security and certainty. We set out on our journey, not knowing what the price of our dream involves or what will be the end result.

Change may burst upon us suddenly and numb us with shock at the enormity of what is happening to our lives. It may be one of a thousand calamities which we have seen affect others, but which we never thought would shatter our own peace so suddenly and cruelly. The change seems like an undeserved disaster from which we will never recover. Yet, if we are to go on living, we have to pick up the pieces and try to put them together again, even though in the beginning we just don't know where to start because everything round us is dark and threatening. These unheralded changes can affect us physically, emotionally and spiritually, so that for a time we seem to disintegrate as persons. The direction of our lives is temporarily taken out of our control when fear engulfs us. Yet if we are to come to terms with what has happened to us, we have to adjust positively to the change affecting us or go under and 'die inside' ourselves. If we are to grow as persons then we must take the suffering in our lives and believe that tomorrow will be a better day when we will know more clearly why such cruel things come our way. It is what we Christians call *trust*.

Unexpected situations, which we can only describe as horrific tragedies, will sometimes arise which will threaten our inner peace and control. No one can prepare for them because they are so enormous and unexpected. Such disasters will not herald their coming, but like an earthquake shake the foundations on which our life is built. On such occasions, our faith will be put to the test and we will need all the help we can get from God as well as the encouragement of those who are closest to us. From the many cases which will help us to understand this, coping with a dramatic, drastic change in our life-style, none is more graphic for me than that of Oliver. He was a normal, successful, happily married man. Life had been good to him and he was very much in control of himself and his life-style. He was a committed Christian and at peace within himself. He was not prepared for what happened to him in his early forties. I asked him to describe it.

'One morning I woke up to find that I was totally and suddenly paralysed from the waist down. I didn't know what it was. Neither did my wife. It was a moment of sheer terror. As soon as the dreadful truth sunk in we sent for the doctor, hoping that it was something temporary. The doctor could not diagnose it, and arranged for me to go straight away to hospital, where for six weeks they did various tests to see if it was a virus or something else. They too failed to come up with a diagnosis. At that juncture my life was bleak. I was afraid I was losing control completely of what was happening and my peace of mind was slipping from me. It was a dark period. I was sent to Stoke Mandeville for six months, after which the doctors were no further forward in the diagnosis of my paralysis. All I knew was that I could not move my legs. I felt so alone I just couldn't face up to my fear. I was told by the doctors that I would spend the rest of my life in a wheel-chair. Elizabeth, my wife, was as shattered as I was. She gave me tremendous help and encouragement. If she had not been at my side, and the person she was, I would not have been able to cope. We came to healing services for our 'spiritual booster'. We see so many others who need help more than we do. We are fortunate that we have so many blessings. In the service we find so much love and compassion among the people that it has given us new insights into our faith. God is helping, so that through him we are in control of the situation and we are not afraid of the future. We have not lost our inner peace since we came to the first healing service. In fact, it has grown!'

Naturally, Oliver would like to walk again and he is right to want that to happen. Because he is confined to a wheelchair he is restricted in his life-style, and we all pray that if it is to God's glory then he will walk again. Oliver, however, is at peace within himself. His faith has conquered his fear of being paralysed. He may not have control over the movement of his legs but he has control of himself. He could be bitter and angry with God and with life, but the overpowering impression that Oliver gives is of a force within him of a living faith which gives him a serenity which is tangible to all who meet him. You may say, 'If this is so, then why pray for his capacity to walk again? Surely it is best to let him be and not build up false hopes? He is paralysed and will always be so. It is a sad case, but this is the end of the story.' But is it?

Such an attitude is totally alien to the Christian gospel. True, Oliver is at peace and in control. He is healed in spirit and he is giving glory to God as he witnesses to his faith, but why not pray for him to be restored in the movement of his legs? Christ prayed for the chalice of his suffering to pass him by and it did not. It is the same with Oliver. He totally accepts his condition. He believes that nothing is impossible to God and, therefore, that God can cure him. Whether he will or not, Oliver still gives glory to God because he is not a fatalist. Like those in the inner healing movement, he believes in miracles. He says that there are others more in need of healing than he is and he is right. There are people paralysed by fear for whom life is a torture chamber, just as there are people devoid of hope and faith who do not believe in miracles. The faith and love of Oliver and Elizabeth are an inspiration to all who meet them. In El Shaddai we pray every day for Oliver and hundreds like him because God would also be glorified if they were cured of their disabilities.

There will be occasions when, unlike the cruel suddenness of what happened to Oliver, good things happen to us as well. Change in our life-style may come gradually and filter softly into our consciousness, much as the light of dawn dispels the darkness of night. Just as a loving parent teaches a child how to walk, so God teaches us how to walk on a new path in our pilgrimage through life.

> I myself taught Ephraim to walk.
> I took them in my arms;
> yet they have not understood that I was the
>   one looking after them.
> I led them with reins of kindness
> with leading-strings of love.
> I was like someone who lifts an infant close
>   against his cheek;
> stooping down to him I gave him his food.
>
> (Hosea 11:3–4)

The events that effect change in us will unfold so gently that we will see things more clearly, moment by moment. We may not fully understand the process as it happens, but in its final outcome we will appreciate that there was a pattern in the changing in which we grew as persons.

This is what happened to David in his pilgrimage in life and it happens to all those who use change creatively and positively as it occurs in their life. David was changed spiritually over quite a long period of time. He responded to the call of the Spirit to change long after he became a minister. He was highly respected by the well-heeled congregation in his comfortable living. His ministry was predictable and was certainly not exciting. I used to visit his area to conduct inner healing services, to which many of his people came. He looked on this as an 'invasion of his territory', an intrusion into his way of conducting his Christian ministry. He saw me as a threat and was forced to do something about it. This is how he described his reaction.

'I soon became aware that what you were saying and doing in your services was affecting some of the most committed people in my congregation. I could sense that they felt they were not being fed by my ministry from the pulpit. That's when I started to hate you and this passed on to the group of your "followers". They knew how I was feeling and reacting towards them, yet they remained peaceful. It was I who was becoming more fearful. Eventually I went along to one of your sessions to discover for myself what happened, but really all I wanted to do was disrupt the meeting. I was uncomfortable from beginning to end and allowed the whole proceedings to go over my head. I vowed never to come again and found solace in like-minded people in my congregation who thought inner healing was all a "flash in the pan", a cult that would disappear. But two months later I came back again to another healing session and at the end I was prepared to admit that the people who came were sincere, even if misguided. I stayed away for six months, but began to feel uneasy in myself that perhaps there was something in inner healing after all. Eventually, I came with an open mind to a healing session in which my whole life changed. We were praying about how difficult it was for Jesus to preach the full gospel of his mission because of the fears of his people. I knew then in a flash that I was afraid of the gospel, and that I fed on the fears of my congregation. I asked for prayers of healing and deep within me I could feel a huge burden being lifted from my heart.

'I could hardly wait for Sunday to tell my people what had happened to me. They knew from the way I spoke that things had changed and so had I. Very soon a deputation came to see me to advise me against continuing my new style of ministry. It was a threat really, but for once in my life I was not afraid. I continued preaching the full gospel of Christ and how we must all be ready to change. I stayed another two years with my people, but few were converted to the way I was preaching the gospel, and so it was obvious that my ministry did not lie with them. It was the Jesus story all over again, when he first preached in his home village. I had to do the same, and so I left for a ministry in another part of the country. Today I am in charge of a smaller congregation, but it is alive and free to worship the Lord in spirit and in truth. I have never been happier. I never realised before how fearful I had become. It is only when the gospel sets you free that you can lose your fear. I feel now, and believe with all my heart, that I am trying to live a truly full and meaningful Christian life. I do not know what the future holds for me but at least now I am ready to face it with a mind and a heart which are free!'

David was content and secure in his role as a minister. The advent of our group threatened his life-style. 'What had we got that he hadn't' was a question he often asked himself. He was so threatened by it that he decided to confront the source of change in his parish, and so he came to our service with a closed mind. He prejudged the issue and decided that he would have none of this inner healing 'gimmick' in his parish. He rationalised the threat to his spiritual life in the company of like-minded people; it is easy to find such comforters among church-goers whenever change is mentioned. Deep down in his heart, however, the question of his ministry still nagged at David, and when it surfaced again two months later, he came in a less destructive mood to another healing service. There he was open enough to see its spiritual value and the effect it had on people's lives.

David reasoned, however, that while it was all right for some, it was not for him or his people. He was a good, sincere man who could have closed the book on healing there and then, but the Spirit was at work on his soul. He

was open enough to appreciate that some of his parishioners were growing through the inner healing
services, and so six months later, after much prayer and
heart-searching, he came with an open mind to our healing service. The Holy Spirit did the rest. David was
released from his bondage. The words of Isaiah were
fulfilled in him. 'He has anointed me to set the captives
free' (Isaiah 61:1). He was no longer afraid of the gospel
or the negative reaction of his people. David was a free
man. His people were not ready for change or for inner
healing, so David moved on to new frontiers and to a new
people. Today his life-style is completely changed. His
living is much more modest, but he is alive and his people
love him because they know he is full of the Spirit in the
best possible sense. His only desire is to stay free as Christ
would have him be. He counts as nothing the sacrifices
he made to follow his dream. He has no regrets about
the past. He had to let his former people go because, like
Abraham, he had been called into a new land. In David,
now well into his sixties, I see the young Christian adven-
turer who responds to the invitation once given to Abraham, 'Leave your country, your family and your father's
house, for the land I will show you. I will make you a
great nation, I will bless you' (Genesis 12:1–2).

The world is full of people like David, if only we look
for them. Inside each one of us there is an ache, a burning
desire, to be free to live our life to the full. For us as
Christians this means exploring the exhilarating gospel
of Jesus which will encourage us to stretch our wings like
an eagle and soar above all the threatening clouds of
doubt and fear which surround change. In my own life, I
have always wanted to be free and the thought of kindred
Christian spirits is my oxygen. It has kept me going. The
ones who have encouraged me most were ordinary people
I met through my Christian ministry of inner healing. In
the face of the most horrendous difficulties, they never
lost their sense of joy in life. Many times I stood in awe

of them and envied their peace of soul. Fear had no part of them because their faith was in control. I think of Jennie who picked up her life again after she was told she had multiple sclerosis. Her husband walked out on her, leaving her with four small children, and all she could think about was how good God was to her and would I please pray for her children that all would go well for them. I remember Charlie, who has terminal cancer. He never complains and always has a smile on his face as he works tirelessly for handicapped children. Then there were John and Beatrice, who lost everything in a financial crash. They said, 'We'll start again, God has been good to us before, he will be good to us again. He is our Father and our peace.' In all these wonderfully brave people, the one golden thread running through their lives, with all their changes, is their unshakeable faith which keeps them full of joy and hope. They are optimists. When faced with problems which would have destroyed other people's lives, they held on to the Christian dream of living life to the full in this life as well as the next. When change came their way they saw it as a challenge to their Christian faith and they were not found wanting. They trusted God as their loving Father who was with them in every moment of their lives, especially when all they had to hold on to was their Christian faith.

Such a person was Philip. Through his crisis he discovered the strength of Christian faith which changed his whole outlook on life. As a result of a car accident, he developed severe spinal trouble. The doctors told him that if he were ever to lead a normal healthy life, then he would require an operation. This involved serious risks: while it might be completely successful, if it went the other way he would become physically immobile and would be confined for the rest of his life to a wheelchair. He received comfort from his wife, family and caring friends, but he knew that ultimately he would have to make up his own mind what to do. But where or how was he to discover the answer? This is how he described his feelings.

'I lived in fear and isolation for months. It is a terrible feeling. I couldn't think straight, could not make a decision. I knew time was running short, but this made me only more desperate, more fearful. My wife had been to many of your healing Masses, but I never came because I'm not a very religious man. My life has not been all that "holy" in the past, and I felt that if God existed then he wouldn't bother too much about a sinner like me. Anyway, my wife persuaded me to come, and so I don't know for what reason, but I came. Mind you, I stayed at the back of the church, well out of range, as I thought, of any healing that might happen! I watched as a spectator and soon I realised how many fearful people there were in church. I could see it on their faces. Then suddenly, here and there, I could sense that there was a power releasing them and setting them free. I was glad for them, but this was not for me. I came again a few times more but always stayed at the back of the church, near the door, so I could make my escape if you approached me with your healing team.

'Then one afternoon when I was feeling very down and fearful I came again to a healing service. As you approached with your team I said in my heart, "Oh God, if you are there please listen to me. I believe you alone can help me. I need your help now." Suddenly I was on my knees and you laid your hands gently on my head and, strangely enough, on my spine and you said, "Courage. Do not be afraid." It was then that the heavy feeling of fear and loneliness left me. In a way which I cannot describe, I knew there was a God and that he cared about me. I buried my head in my hands and I cried in relief. I knew God would supply the answer. Today I am a different person. I am much happier and at peace within myself. My fears are gone and the doctors tell me now that I do not need to have the operation. Has my peace of body and soul changed my physical condition? I don't know, but I know that God will look after me no matter what happens to me in the rest of my life. My faith has deepened and the terrible fear which was destroying my life has lost its hold over me.'

Philip was cured as well as healed. I believe from my contact with him that if he had had the operation and it had gone wrong he would still be blessed with faith to grow through the situation. Why some people and not others are cured is a mystery which I have never understood, especially where young, innocent children are concerned. I have encountered hundreds of people who find their suffering hard to accept and are so burdened by their sorrow that they cannot seem able to emerge into the daylight which hope brings. It is here that their faith is put to the test and we must encourage them to keep on believing and hoping that the clouds will disappear and that once again they will find inner peace and happiness.

David, Philip and Oliver were healed because they were open to change. They were converted. The Hebrew word for conversion is *shuba*, which means changing direction. This is the message of Jesus, who said, 'I am the way': we have to change direction and follow him. The more fixed people are in their ways and modes of thinking, the more difficult it is for them to accept even the smallest alteration to the *status quo*. They will not countenance any suggestion that yesterday's problems or solutions are irrelevant to today's world and people. They will not move on in their thinking because they refuse to accept that they have not yet arrived at their destination, even though where they are is only a station in their journey through life.

If we really want to use changes in our lives creatively, then we must have a positive attitude and not worry unduly about them. We have to live one day at a time. By all means we should work out how we are going to cope in the future if we are facing a terrible calamity, but we have to take life as it is now. Tomorrow it may be worse, but it could also be better. We are not to overload ourselves. Jesus reminds us that 'each day has enough troubles of its own' (Matthew 6:34). In my own life, I have come to believe that the God who looked after me yesterday will look after me tomorrow if only I learn to trust him. I now see my life as having a thread running through it. My work for peace in Northern Ireland, which began in such pain after my ministry in my pastoral centre was abruptly terminated, found its fuller meaning in the healing ministry. I believe that God was equally present all the time in each venture, even though I was not fully conscious of it at the time. He had his plan for me and to be part of it I had to grow through the pain which the changes involved. God knows our problems and difficulties in all the changes that take place in our lives, so we do not have to carry the burden alone. God as our Father will change the situation because he will change us so that the crisis becomes a point of personal growth. 'I am no longer trying for perfection by my own efforts,' writes St Paul, 'the perfection that comes from the Law, but I want only the perfection that comes through faith in Christ, and is from God and is based on faith.' (Philippians 3:9)

Change may at times threaten our peace, but it should never destroy it. When we learn to take all our problems to the Lord, then we will experience the truth of his words: 'Come to me, all you who labour and are overburdened, and I will give you rest.' (Matthew 11:28) We cannot solve all our problems alone. We need help, not only from friends, but also from a higher source. I have found from my experience in the El Shaddai ministry that far too many people suffer alone and cannot cope with the changes in their lives, especially those caused by the suffering of their loved ones. We all need to support one another, especially in our families.

Take the case of James. One day he was rushed to hospital after a suspected overdose. The suspicion proved to be false, but not before he had had his stomach pumped. This procedure resulted in a deprivation of oxygen and subsequent brain damage. At first his parents were convinced that their son was going to die. James lay in a coma while his life hung in the balance. The whole family took it in turn to stay by his bedside day and night for the next few weeks, dreading the worst. The weeks turned into months and James' condition stabilised as much as it was ever going to. He has been in this condition for eight years. His eyes are open and he responds minimally to sound, but to all intents and purposes he is 'dead'. The effect on the family has been extraordinary. They have tended to all James' needs and this has brought them closer together as a family, even though they do not understand God's will which allowed such a calamity to happen to one so young. His father attends to him lovingly – he has given him a bath and a shave every day for the past eight years – while another member of the family helps out on two days in order to give the father a break. They are grateful for the nursing staff and friends, in whom they have seen the caring Christ. Their chief support has been their belief in God the Father who in a thousand and one different ways has shown his love for each and every one of them. It is his love which has drawn them together so that they can cope with the tragedy of James' illness. They still pray for James' cure because for them while there is life there is hope. They pray for the miracle of James' recovery, but the real miracle is the strengthening of their love and their faith and hope in each other and in God.

James may seem a hopeless case. I do not share that view and neither do his family. They believe that nothing is impossible to God. They live in hope that he will be cured one day, while at the same time their feet are still firmly on the ground. Hope in God often begins where hope in human effort ends. I believe that many people threatened by terminal illness, alcoholism, gambling or any other debilitating factor must never say that their situation is hopeless. Life without hope is not life at all. *People are not dying of cancer; they are living with it.* This affirmation of life brings a quality to their lives which in itself is a great healing, not only for themselves but for those they love. The optimist lives each day to the full not because he may not have a tomorrow, but because it is the best way to prepare for living tomorrow. Living one day at a time is the true Christian approach to any problem we encounter during the day itself. Every morning I say a prayer (from *The Treasury of the Holy Spirit*) for my inner peace of mind and heart which no event of the day may destroy:

> Father, take this day of my life into your safe and loving care, so that I may live each moment to the full in peace and gladness. May I never lose your presence in any distraction that the day may bring, but remember always that you are closer to me than my own breathing, as present and life-giving as every beat of my heart. May each breath I take and each heartbeat I make, deepen my awareness of your presence and love.

I know that the only way I can really live with all the changes which the day may bring is when I am at peace within myself. It was not always so. There were times when I woke up in the morning, dreading what the day would bring. It brought my life to a standstill because an inordinate fear of change had taken control of my life. Because I came through it with God's help, I can in some small way encourage others to see change in their lives in a positive Christian way. Many suffer far more than I did, but at least I can try to identify with them.

People today are probably more insecure than they were a few decades ago. The break-up of marriages, lack of job security, the need to travel to unfamiliar places to find work, all contribute to a feeling of being lost in an alien world. There is no escape. We cannot return to the world of yesterday which gave us security and a feeling of belonging. Today's world may seem far harsher, more violent and impersonal. If ever we needed our Christian faith to conquer our fear of change, then it is today. In a changing world the rock on which our life is built is our faith in God our Father whom we trust with our life and all its changes. He will make all things new (Revelation 21:5). The vision of hope before our eyes is that in all the changes which happen to us in life he is healing us.

7

Afraid to Know and Love Yourself

Uncontrolled fear is the enemy within which destroys our inner peace and takes away our freedom. It prevents us from knowing and loving ourselves. Because it wants to control us, it inhibits us from trying to discover who we really are, and what, if any, is our purpose in life. If we never get to know who we are, then how can we love ourselves? And if we don't love ourselves then love can have no part in our lives. We become loveless, lifeless people. This is exactly what uncontrolled fear, our enemy, wants. I know this is true of my own life. It was only when I became aware of what uncontrolled fear could do to me that I was able to confront it and grow as a person. With God's help there is no way that I am ever again going to allow fear to take away my inner peace and dominate my life.

I know only too well that fear is the enemy of personal freedom and growth in inner peace. Fearful people go through life growing old but never growing up. Fear dwarfs our personality. It warns us against too much self-examination because it tells us that in the final analysis we will not like what we find, and end up rejecting ourselves. For the fearful, ignorance is bliss. To some extent I used to be like that. I accepted far too easily what people said and thought of me. I didn't think enough for, or of, myself. It just wasn't done to ask too many questions of my peers.

The total conformist is fear's most obedient servant.

He is not free, and therefore not human. Fearful people live on the surface because the world and its institutions do not like people to be free! The reactions of fearful people are predictable. They are so controlled that when a crisis comes in their lives they are unable to cope with it. They blame others for their own failure to have the courage to face up to reality. The fault, however, lies not in their stars nor in others but in themselves. If they learn any lesson from the challenge to self which a crisis brings, it is to avoid such crises in the future. Fear makes us opt for pseudo-stability and security which will allow nothing to rock the boat. Loyalty to the group, the community, the institution, is their criterion. Love has a much lower priority.

God meant us to be ourselves, to grow in freedom and true love of the person we are as we reach out in hope to the person we want to become. Each day I know that if I am true to myself I shall grow as a person. God understands my weaknesses and fears. He leaves me free to grow because he knows that in freedom lies my only hope of being more fully human, happy and alive. Jesus, from the age of twelve until he was thirty, lived in Nazareth with Mary and Joseph where he 'increased in wisdom, in stature and in favour with God and men' (Luke 2:52). Jesus grew as a person in the freedom of his own home and village. You and I are God's children, and he wants us to grow as persons in our own situations. We will never achieve this if we allow fear to dominate our thinking and way of living. We will not grow in our personal relationship with God and other people. Why? Because fear will isolate us, cut us off on our own little island of self-centredness. This is a recipe for emotional and spiritual disaster.

If we live only for ourselves then ultimately we will only have ourselves to live with. We will never love ourselves as we are. Truth suffers, so does prophecy, as the world becomes the poorer while we all play our own unreal games in our isolated unrelated groups. Yet the great need in our world is for reality and truth, and for people to love themselves as they are without all the artificial trimmings which act as a disguise preventing even they themselves from knowing who they are. When image becomes the important thing in people's lives and society then there is a crisis of identity. We cease to be persons, and become ciphers in an inhuman materialistic system.

It is only when I am in control of fear that I am able to be at peace within myself. Once I know who I am and what I am capable of, I shall acknowledge my weaknesses as well as my strengths. I shall be true to myself and this is what everyone should want to be. I shall not be a Walter Mitty or a Uriah Heap. I shall know and love myself in a truly human, Christian way. Then I shall have got the right balance in my life because I shall have learned to use fear correctly. I shall control it rather than allow it to control me. Fear, when it is controlled by my Christian faith and love, helps me to use my freedom sensitively, wisely and courageously so that I grow as a person. It warns me when I am tempted to take false liberties with myself or others. I use true love of self and genuine fear as a barometer for inner peace. They help me to know and love myself correctly. Self-discovery and self-love are absolutely necessary for me if I want to use the right controls in my life. There is no other way. Then I shall know what I should or should not do in order to grow in peace as a person. I shall try to take my Christian standards from the life of Christ and not be guided by the false principles of a materialistic world. To be in control and at peace is Christ's gift to me. If anyone is to be in control of me it will be the Holy Spirit who loves me and wants what is best for me. I am not going to settle for a second-best. It will take me a lifetime to grow in my knowledge and awareness of myself as a person. I have made many mistakes in my life either by under-valuing or over-estimating my potential. I hope that today I am a wiser person. When I did not know or love myself correctly then things got out of control in my life. Fear took over on those occasions and gave me a false picture of myself. I was slow to appreciate the truth of the situation because I was too interested in my own image. I did not acknowledge what was happening because fear was in control and it did not allow me to. I had to re-examine the situation and get back on the track if I wanted the right kind of control in my life. This was always a painful process and gradually led me into Christian healing. When I was in a spiritual and emotional desert, preoccupied with licking my wounds and feeling sorry for myself, I realised I had to change. It gradually dawned on me that working for peace in Northern Ireland would not be solved by my efforts alone or those of like-minded people, but by God's healing power. The only way to peace in Northern Ireland was, and is, when people would allow God to change their hearts and attitudes. This was the path to peace and the changing had to begin with me. This change set me on the road to the ministry of healing, so out of the chaos of a dangerous and destructive situation my life of true inner peace and healing began.

When inordinate fear rules our lives then the words 'in control' take on a completely new meaning. They have strong overtones of power. The true Christian power I have within myself is to be at peace and to grow as a person. But there is another form of power which is destructive not only of ourselves but of others. We want to be in control of other people. This is the worst form of the corruption of power. Institutions need to be wary of the danger because they are often composed of damaged people who get themselves into a position of power and control, which they then use to their own advantage and self-aggrandisement. They stand on higher ground because we choose to live in valleys. The corruption began when others so under-valued themselves in their own eyes that they allowed the worldly ambitious people to take over and control their lives. I have always tried to fight against this because of the havoc it causes in people's lives, but there are relatively few who are prepared to stand up and be counted for what they believe is true and right. Jesus did and so should we, but we are afraid of the consequences.

People and situations can so threaten and control us that we lose control of ourselves. It prevents us from being the people we know we are or want to be. We are in the grip of fear which controls our spirit. We tend to look over our shoulders at those 'over' us in order to gauge their reaction and seek their approval. We never think or act for ourselves. We play subservient roles because this is what is expected of us. Yet Jesus never asked for such an attitude from his disciples. He wants us to be free because only then are we able to be ourselves and control fear. The most precious thing we possess is our freedom. Without it we would not be human. When we act automatically in conformity with others without thinking for ourselves, then we are robots. Power, or being in control of people, will always crush the individual who questions its authority or decisions. Such power is not only corrupting of those who wield it but also of those who subject themselves to it. It is the enemy of change, except in those things which will increase its power. Whenever I feel threatened by power-orientated people and situations I distance myself from them in order to maintain my peace. Of course I speak out when my conscience tells me that it is my Christian duty to do so, but I leave the outcome to God. Many of us suffer spiritual leukaemia and we need massive injections of faith and courage in witnessing to the truth of the Christian gospel in all its aspects.

God created us free. Everyone has a right to freedom. In our healing services we constantly stress the need to love ourselves in such a way that no one can usurp our innate dignity as persons. Inner peace is a human right which as Christians we should uphold as much as any other form of human liberty. We can be prisoners within ourselves in a cage of fear just as much as in a gaol made of bricks and bars. Fear can bind us and only faith in a God who loves us will set us totally free. Failure to love ourselves is the main cause of fear controlling us. It cripples so many people that I wonder how on earth they got into such a state. I can achieve little in ministering healing to anyone who is chained in fear. I try to unlock their chains by encouraging these unhappy people to believe in themselves, that they are lovable and of great value. I let them know that if I love them and want them to be free how much more God their Father loves them. After all he sent his son Jesus 'to preach liberty to the captives'. But teaching them that God wants them to be in control of their peace is a very slow and painful process because they have been so damaged by life. It takes years, even a lifetime, to readjust the balance but the end result is well worth the effort. It is a joy to see people so changed in themselves that they are free to enjoy life. For them their healing is a resurrection. It is as precious as giving sight to the blind.

I could tell you countless stories of people whose lives were so controlled by fear that they did not really live. Margaret was one of them. She was in a most distressed state when she first came to one of our healing services. She looked dejected and beaten by life. She was completely withdrawn within herself and her response to what I hope was our sensitive approach to her was like trying to get a spark out of a dead car battery. Life had aged and scarred her. She said that her home life was completely loveless and negative. She had no friends, lived alone, and had been unemployed for over ten years. She struggled through her daily existence with stooped shoulders as if expecting even worse disasters to befall her. There was no life, no hope, no joy in her. She was deeply religious in that she never missed her weekly Mass and yet when I spoke to her of God's love for her she gave a deep sigh of hopelessness as she told me resignedly that all her trouble came from a God who wished to punish her for her sins. Fear of God controlled her life. When I asked her what she wanted from God she remained silent. Actually she came to the service for healing, but she neither expected it nor, I suspect, wanted it. There was no remedy for her misery. It was all she had ever known.

When I started to pray for her so that she would be healed as a person in the whole of her life, I took her hand gently. It was cold. I discerned that she was in the grip of fear which was controlling her. She gave me no reaction, but I knew in my heart that Margaret would return again for healing. At the next service I prayed gently with her again and told her that she did not love herself and that this was the main blockage in her life. She told me that while it was true that she did not love herself she saw no reason to do so. She never looked on God as a father. It took many further sessions before Margaret began to come alive. There were times when I could cheerfully have called it a day, but eventually her faith began to grow and her fear diminish. It was a hard battle. She would recover for a while and then go back again to her defeatist attitude to life. When it is in control for such a long time fear does not easily release its grip. However, after seven long years Margaret is on the road to recovery. Today she is able to make friends, has a very fulfilling job and also does voluntary work which gives her a great sense of helping others. She is still scarred by her previous life, but now she understands why. She comes to as many healing services as she can, because, she says, she needs them if she is to keep her old self from taking her over again. Margaret is alive and growing as a person. The process will last a lifetime.

Surely it goes without saying that if our love for ourselves is to be true, as Jesus' love was, then it must change and grow with the passing of time through different people and situations. Our values as a child are not the same as they will become as an adolescent. We grow through our experiences. As we become older we will be constantly reassessing our attitude to life and to ourselves. We are changing every day. All through our lives at every stage, we have to find a corresponding valid reason for loving ourselves. This reason should so penetrate and permeate every aspect of our life that in whatever circumstances we find ourselves this genuine love of self will never be diminished or destroyed. In fact it will grow.

There will be times when we will discover that we are not as good a person as we thought we were. There will also be occasions when hitherto unknown powers of hidden strength within us will express themselves in such a way that we will grow in an awareness of ourselves as persons. Little by little we will begin to know ourselves better, warts and all. By all means we must be objective and self-critical, but in the bad times we should never lose sight of the fact that we are still lovable and that our lives have a purpose. At those times we need to look on the positive side of ourselves as well, and become aware of our strong points. We must never undervalue our true worth. This is what uncontrolled fear wants us to do.

It is easy to love yourself when everything is going well and everyone is on your side, but the real love of self shows itself for its true value when everything seems to be going wrong and those nearest and dearest to us seem to distance themselves from us. It is a time not only when we come to know who our real friends are but when we realise how deeply we need to value ourselves so that we may grow more fully as persons. This is the best, perhaps only, way to retain our inner peace and control our fears. Every crisis is a growing point in our life and our journey of self-discovery and self-acceptance.

Cecil is a typical case of people we meet in our healing ministry. He was pretty successful in business, seemed happily married, and was readily accepted socially by a large circle of friends. Then suddenly the company for which he worked, once so secure, went bankrupt, and Cecil's stability was shattered. However hard he tried, he just could not find suitable alternative employment. He began to lose confidence in himself and soon, because of his financial embarrassment, he was unable to maintain his previous social standards. His 'friends' gradually melted away out of his life. His wife, Patricia, stood by him, but his children were too young to realise what was happening to their father. Cecil tells us of the depths of his despair, and how his faith conquered the fear that was destroying him, so that eventually he was able to recover the deep inner peace which he had lost during his crisis period. This is what he wrote:

'I was disintegrating as a person. I saw no hope for the future, and the fear of what might happen to us as a family disturbed my sleeping and waking hours. In fact, I just could not sleep. I was afraid that soon we would lose the home we loved so much because we could not meet the mortgage. But more than that I began to hate and blame myself for the trouble I had brought on those I loved. I was so afraid of each day's dawn that I drew in on myself completely. I saw no purpose in life. I lost my peace of mind. I felt too that I was losing my faith in God.

'Then one day I went to a healing service in which the whole message was that God loved us as only a true Father could. The theme of the service was that no matter what happened to us, or what difficulties we were in, God's love for us was constant. He would never fail to give us what we needed most – love and courage to live life to the full even, or especially, in the bad times when nothing seems to go right for us as we look at the future in gloom and fear. The reading from the Bible at the healing service that day was the letter of St Paul to the Romans, Chapter 8, verses 31–39. The words touched me at the service and lifted me up. Today my life is changed. My relationship with Patricia and the children has deepened and we are a happier family now than we have ever been. I know God is my loving Father, not only in my head but also in my heart. Fear does not rule my life and I feel as free as the birds in the air because I know I have a reason for loving myself. My greatest wealth is to know and to love myself as a person whom God loves. I know myself better now than I did before I lost my job.'

For Cecil, and for us as Christians, the ultimate reason why we love and are at peace with ourselves, is because God loved us first and keeps on loving us no matter what changing situations we may find ourselves in. Our faith in God's abiding love for us as a Father was clearly shown when he sent his Son into our world to become one of us in human flesh. His Son shares our life and our problems no matter how tiny or gigantic they may be. God never fails to love us in his risen and ascended Son. No matter what happens or what unexpected catastrophe befalls us, we have the resurrection, the greatest reason, the strongest rock, on which to base our true love of self and our reason for joy and hope.

Our living faith in the Father's love for us in Christ conquers every fear and brings us deep inner peace. Fear which wants to control us cannot share the same person with deep living Christian faith. We believe that if God gave us his Son then he will not refuse us anything we need in order to become more fully human, more fully alive. This is what touched Cecil's life and changed him. The text of St Paul which helped him will surely help you also.

> With God on our side who can be against us? Since God did not spare his own Son, but gave him up to benefit us all, we may be certain, after such a gift, that he will not refuse anything he can give. Could anyone accuse those that God has chosen? When God acquits, could anyone condemn? Could Christ Jesus? No! He not only

died for us – he rose from the dead, and there at God's right hand he stands and pleads for us.

Nothing therefore can come between us and the love of Christ, even if we are troubled or worried, or being persecuted, or lacking food or clothes, or being threatened or even attacked. As scripture promised: For your sake we are being massacred daily, and reckoned as sheep for the slaughter. These are the trials through which we triumph, by the power of him who loved us.

For I am certain of this: neither death nor life, no angel, no prince, nothing that exists, nothing still to come, not any power, or height or depth, nor any created thing, can ever come between us and the love of God made visible in Christ Jesus our Lord. (Romans 8:31–39)

In return for this total love of us by God in Christ, which, if only we have faith, we will find all around us, we are to love ourselves and our neighbour, and be glad that we are alive, living every day to the full, one day at a time. This awareness of God's love for us rarely happens instantly. It grows, and as it does, fear correspondingly diminishes. This may all sound idealistic and pie-in-the-sky, but as the years roll on I find it increasingly true in my own life. I believe that trials only come to test us and to help us to be aware of the hidden power for good within us, enabling us to grow as free, joyful persons.

Our faith in God's love for us helps us to see above and beyond the clouds of doubt and uncertainty which oppress us. We shall overcome, whatever the situation. The Christian way of loving ourselves frees us from the entangled web of the destructive forces of uncontrolled fear. And yet the vast majority of people, or so it seems to me, do not love themselves for who or what they are. They feel they have 'to be somebody', to be successful, if they are to be loved. The insidious force of overpowering fear, the opposite of love, gets a foothold in their way of thinking and acting whenever things go wrong in their lives.

Why does this happen? The simple answer is that when crises come we do not believe in God as a loving Father because we do not believe in or love ourselves. We cannot accept the fact that there is anything lovable in our real selves so we play games with masks on. We are afraid to be ourselves because we have not the courage to investigate what kind of person we really are. We do not believe that we can overcome the crisis which confronts us and so we capitulate without a struggle. Uncontrolled fear wins the war without a battle. We dare not search the hidden parts of our personality lest, when they are discovered, they may threaten us with the stark reality of our naked, cowardly selves which we refuse to love or accept. We engage in self-excuse, and promise never again to explore the deep recesses of our personality.

Uncontrolled fear makes us hide the skeleton of our true selves in our cupboards. We become 'externalised' people living on the periphery of life so that we avoid those situations which confront us with ourselves. Yet until we have the courage to face up to who we really are, in difficult and even frightening situations, we will never come alive as persons. We cannot be happy on the outside without first being happy on the inside. This may sound like a cliché but it is very true for each one of us. To be genuine, happiness must flood the whole person inside and outside, and we will never be happy unless we are at peace within ourselves.

Roger reinforces what I mean about not being afraid to continue your search for the real you. His case is similar to Cecil's. Roger is a successful businessman in his late forties whom everyone seems to regard as a very complete, very rounded person. He is rarely to be found in bad humour or depressed. Nothing seems to get him down. And yet this is nothing other than 'surface happiness' because what Roger actually thinks within himself is quite the opposite.

'I really do not know who or what I am. I have accepted the social standards of the world round me in order to find my niche in society. I think I have done well. I like going to parties and enjoying myself. Most people seem to think I have a terrific sense of humour and am great fun! Deep down I feel there is another "me" which wants a fuller life which I need to express, and which would bring me real inner peace, but I'm afraid of the consequence involved. There is also another "me" which is quite violent and would like to destroy all round me as a sham. I've settled for the middle course, but the old skeletons rattle inside me all the time, and I have got even more fearful in recent years, nearly to bursting point. I'm afraid that one day the "wrong me" will break out.'

One of the factors which helped Roger to be healed of his irrational fear was his awareness that all of us are a mixture inside of all sorts of strange 'characters' and that God understands not only who and what we are, but what we might be. We are not to be afraid of what we find because God has loved it first and healed it through his Son. Roger's Christian faith calmed his fears so that he could live at peace within himself, knowing that when the worst came to the worst, Christ would be there telling him that he had won the victory over his 'wicked' self.

Over the years Roger found deep inner peace within himself and learned to live a more fulfilled, more peaceful life. I have found that the text of Romans 2:14–25 has a very special healing power for people like Roger. I suggest that if you are like him then you should read them often, especially whenever fear begins to rear its ugly head to threaten your peace. I have encountered many people like Roger in our healing sessions, for whom a prayer from *The Treasury of the Holy Spirit* (page 211) has a special significance:

I thank thee, Lord, for knowing me better than I know myself, and for letting me know myself better than others know me. Make me, I pray, better than they suppose, and forgive me for what they do not know.

Instead of loving ourselves in a truly positive Christian way we often pray, 'Lord, deliver us from ourselves' without ever giving ourselves a chance to become the kind of person God wants us to become. The reason is obvious. We are not in love with who we are, and we believe that in the final analysis we are basically unlovable. How or why God loves us – if we really believe it – will remain a mystery, and we put it down to his mercy rather than to anything of value in ourselves. We reject in practice, although perhaps not consciously, God's creation in us. We consider that we are part of the sin and ugliness of the world, and so we limp through life without ever coming to grips with the reality which is the 'me' in each of us. Fear has so controlled us that we have only a partial knowledge of ourselves.

Our love of ourselves, like our knowledge of God, is limited. We try to hide who we are from God, from others and above all from ourselves in the wilderness of the world we have made around us because of our inordinate, uncontrolled fear. 'Where are you?' God asks. 'I heard the sound of you in the garden.' We reply, 'I was naked and so I hid.' 'Who told you that you were naked?' God asks, and we have no reply. Fear has driven us into a situation of our own making. Because we have failed to come to terms with ourselves in a crisis we play the deadly destroying game of hide-and-seek with life, with God and with ourselves. We prefer the façade of religion to the reality of faith. Religion is shallow and comforts us. Faith takes us into uncharted waters of the deep, and we don't want to take the risks of the challenges involved. We settle for second best, a religion without faith, a life without love.

Despite our calmness on the surface, like Roger we are still basically disturbed because the question of personal identity – 'Who am I?' – remains unanswered. We never really square up to the question because we are afraid of the answer we might get. So we remain locked in on ourselves through irrational fear, and the 'real self' becomes even more frustrated as we refuse it an outlet for expression. We are at war within ourselves, which is the perfect recipe for neurosis. Religion, like a drug, becomes our tranquilliser so that we can maintain an even keel in the troublesome sea which we have made of life. Tranquillisers never make for tranquillity. The sad thing is that we delude ourselves so that we become addicted to our spiritual rocking chair which helps us to 'rest' when we are restless. Our calm is on the surface, while underneath the tensions build up to breaking point. Deep down in our minds and hearts we are aware of the undercurrents beneath the surface and we expect the storm to blow up any minute and destroy the frail boat of self which we knew all along would never make it across the sea of life.

In over forty-four years of ministering to people, I have found that failure to be their true selves is the main cause of loneliness and despair in our world. It is the chief source of nervous breakdowns and deep unhappiness. The fear to be ourselves is the most difficult emotion to control because we do not know of what we are afraid. Yet irrational fear has to be faced up to and dragged out of the dark places where it lurks. It has taken over territory that does not belong to itself. It is a squatter in our home, whom we are afraid to evict because of what might happen. It is the 'unknown' into which we must enter with the light of faith. Fear recedes as the light of faith illuminates the interior and shows us what a mess fear is making of our lives. When we see, in its proper light, what fear is doing to our lives then we will appreciate what battles lie ahead if we are to have a true, authentic personal identity and proper appreciation of ourselves. An enemy confronted is less terrible than unseen forces which, lurking in the background, steadily erode our self-confidence. It is the obscure menace which unnerves the mind. The nameless dread is put before us in a startling way in Coleridge's haunting image in 'The Rime of the Ancient Mariner':

> Like one, that on a lonesome road
> Doth walk in fear and dread
> And having once turned round walks on
> And turns no more his head;
> Because he knows a frightful fiend
> Doth close behind him tread.

Our greatest irrational fear is to recognise ourselves for what we are, lest not only are we rejected by others, but that we too reject what we find. Self-rejection is destructive of any kind of personal growth. Self-analysis is a pain we would rather be without. So we look on life as a dark menace which will engulf us in some future inevitable calamity. We think that the seeds of destruction are within us, and so we are afraid that they may grow one day to such proportions as to smother all the things in life that we hold dear. We shrink from darkness and the elemental fear of being left totally alone: 'with darkness my one companion left' (Psalm 88).

A typical example of this 'masking ourselves from ourselves', because of the fear of self-rejection, is Brian. I have met hundreds like him whose work and busy social life distract them from sitting down and having a good look at themselves. Brian is a civil engineer whose business prospered even at times when people in the same profession were experiencing a slump. It was the same all through his life. His academic achievements at college and university were considerable and everything he touched was successful. He was happily married, with a loving family. Then, in his late forties, he started having self-doubts about the quality of his work, his motivation, his attitude to his wife and family and, strangely enough for someone who was deeply religious, about his faith in a loving God. He fell to pieces and no amount of reassuring him of how good and kind he was to everyone all through his life seemed to heal him. He fell ever deeper into depression and became a source of worry to those who loved him dearly.

Eventually, after much prayer and soul-searching, he acknowledged that he had never looked at himself deep inside because he was afraid of what he might find. First with Brian, and afterwards with his wife, we were able to help him discover who he really was. 'Today,' he says, 'I am not afraid of who I am, and I don't want to be anyone else. There are times when the fear of self-doubt rears its ugly head, but I know how to deal with it now. I may not be perfect, but I am "me" and I know God loves me. I am really at peace within myself, I live one day at a time. The future holds no fears for me because, like the past, I have committed it into the hands of God my Father who knows and loves me.'

A very great help in fighting fear is not merely to ask ourselves the questions, 'What am I afraid of in myself?' and 'Why?', but to write down the questions and answers for future reflection and action. Fear hates to be confronted since it lives by innuendo and unspoken menace. It is the question mark which becomes the tombstone over our buried self. Like a vampire it sucks our life blood so that we have to unearth the coffin, open it and drive a stake, made of faith and belief in ourselves and God's love for us, through the heart of the demon fear. Only then will we find peace and the freedom to live our lives to the full. Once we know our secret fears for what they are, we can set about finding a remedy. Psychiatric help may be sought in exploring the subconscious and laying bare the origin of the things which stunt our human growth. But while psychology helps us to overcome some fears, particularly those that are abnormal and phobic, nevertheless what we are really lacking in life is faith – faith in ourselves and faith in God.

How does irrational fear take us over? It invades us in a thousand and one different ways. Its source is as unique as the individual who is its victim. It may enter through the body, mind or soul of the person, but it affects the person as a whole. It refuses to accept any boundaries, and is by nature aggressive. This is why it has to be tackled immediately, as soon as the first symptoms are discovered. If we are so precautionary about cancer and other diseases, then why do we not treat fear in the same way? Irrational fear can make us think that we suffer from all sorts of physical and emotional disorders.

Take the case of Janet. She went constantly to doctors, convinced she had a growth in her stomach. She had innumerable tests which were negative, but she would not accept that everything was normal and that she had nothing to worry about. Eventually, discounting the doctors as pretty useless, she went to psychiatrists for treatment, but all to no avail. Her life came to a standstill, and she was forced to give up her employment. She had her 'up and down' days, but hardly a day went by without her inordinate fear engulfing her in some form of crisis over her state of health. She stayed in bed for days on end, and her life seemed to have lost all its vitality and meaning. When she was brought by friends to our healing session I was quite shocked at her appearance. She looked like a skeleton and had all the external symptoms of someone in great physical pain and distress. She was so filled with fear that we could do little or nothing for her at the first two healing sessions. Gradually, however, we got her to look at herself through God's loving eyes, and to understand that he believed in her even if she did not believe in herself. We showed her how her fears were imaginary. Through God's grace she was healed of her fears which had been with since childhood. Today she has some very good friends to whom she can relate extremely well, and she has part-time employment in which she meets and helps people. This draws her out of herself. Occasionally she lapses back into moods of deep fear, but this is soon checked through prayer and the help of understanding friends. When fear knocks at her door she opens it in faith to find no one there but a loving, caring Father who wants to come into the home of her heart and fill the void of her loneliness with his love.

What I am repeating in this book time and again is that the greatest antidote to fear is to love yourself and to believe that God is your loving Father who never stops supporting and loving you. This belief in God and yourself comes through faith and not through religion. Religion touches the exterior of our personality. Faith in God's love for us reaches the innermost depths of our being. It is this faith alone which brings us inner peace. We cannot possibly be at peace with others until we have learned to be at peace with ourselves. So we have to learn to live with, and by, the fact that God loves us with his love – God's love for us rather than our love for him. This is the measure of our love for ourselves. I know it is easier said than done, but until we begin to act in the light of this great truth, we will never be healed of irrational fear. We will never discover ourselves by our own resources.

Many people travel across the world in an attempt to discover their roots. Our journey of self-discovery is the most difficult journey we will ever undertake. It is a journey which begins and ends with ourselves. The search for oneself is really our search for God. Only he can light up our lives and lead us gently on the path to self-discovery. Then, and only then, will we really begin to know who we are. The bonds of inordinate fear will be broken and we will at last be free to be ourselves. There is no greater freedom.

8

Fear Destroys Hope and Joy

Fear, when we allow it to control our lives, breeds misery. Fearful people have little joy in their lives. Happiness is something which never seems to come their way. For them life is an agony, a real pain. They even regret being born. They never look forward to the future with any great optimism – in fact, the opposite. They dread the future because life for them is a tortuous series of misfortunes which can only get worse. Life has a nasty irreversible habit of playing dirty tricks on them. The clouds which surround their lives never have a silver lining. Life becomes darker, more confined and miserable, as the years roll relentlessly and slowly on. The rainbow of hope is a fantasy, something they have never experienced. Devoid of hope, they see no purpose or direction in their lives. The momentum in their lives, such as it is, soon grinds to a halt. What is the point of hoping, they say, if everything is going to end in failure and unhappiness?

We have all met such people. Brenda's life-style before she came to inner healing services, is a perfect example of a person devoid of hope and joy. The healing services were in fact only the beginning of her healing as a person. The process took a long time and was very painful for her. Here is how she describes her attitude to life:

'For as long as I can remember I never got any joy out of life and I have no happy memories of my childhood. My parents never showed me any real affection. I suppose that is why I could never make friends with anyone. They said I was a loner, but in fact I just felt worthless in myself. No one seemed to want to be my friend. I suppose I should have made the effort, but I was afraid of rejection. My brothers and sisters seemed to be able to do everything. They were achievers. I achieved nothing. While they made friends, I sulked alone in a corner. I was lonely, but I hadn't the courage to tell anyone how I really felt. I hated school. The other children teased me unmercifully, but that was better than being ignored. I hated the playground because I couldn't join in their laughter or games. I spent recreation time in the toilet.

'When I left school I knew it would only be for the worse. I was right. I got a job but hated that even more than being at school. In the evenings after work, I never went anywhere or did anything, the reason being that if ever I took up any hobby it soon fell to pieces because of failed relationships. I was constantly away from work on sick leave because I dreaded facing the others on the staff. The inevitable happened. My services were no longer required! Soon I was on the shuttle between the doctor and psychiatrist. They changed my pills, but not me. I was dead inside and often wanted to end my life, but that was for me a cowardly way out. My parents died. My brothers and sisters, who had all married by then, had given up on me. I know what depression is. What I had to live with was more destructive and painful than any form of depression.

When I was at my lowest ebb, a person from the church told me there was a healing service on that afternoon. She collected me and brought me, otherwise I would not have gone. Strange, but I never missed weekly Mass, to which I went out of a sense of duty. There was no joy, no uplift in it. I intended to sit through the healing service as bored as I usually was at Sunday worship. The healing service was different. The people there seemed happy and much more alive than our usual Sunday congregations. I heard you talk about God the Father's love for me as a person. This, you said, was the one thing that really mattered. I was only half-listening, so the message didn't really sink in until you came to the pew I was in and called me out. You said something to me that has stayed with me over the years. 'God is your Father,' you said, 'and you are special to him. Never mind what others think. You love yourself because you are unique. God your Father believes in you. You need to learn to believe in yourself.' Then you put your hands on my head, and for the first time in my life I felt special to someone, and then the tears began to flow. I just couldn't control them. I didn't know whether they were tears of joy, self-pity or what. All I knew was that I was being released from the prison I had made of my life. After that I came many times to the healing services and gradually my life has changed.

It was a slow process, but it was worth it. Before the healing services I was afraid to live and afraid to end my life. Now for me, after all these years of self-torture, life is just beginning. I never look back to the past any more. I can't change what has happened. But I can look forward to the future because I can do something about that. I am free to help others who feel unloved and useless because I have been down that dark and dreary path myself. My life has a purpose. I hope I am a more joyful person than I was because I know now that life is really worth living!'

Like Brenda we all need large doses of hope which makes us glad to be alive. Unless we see a purpose in life then what is the point of living? If our attitude to life is miserable then we will not bother to get up in the morning to face another gruelling day. Brenda did not believe in herself as a person, and because of this she did not believe in anyone else. She did not really believe in God, and certainly did not look on him as her loving Father. Brenda's first step in her inner healing came when she began to know and experience God. We prayed first of all that the experience of God's presence which she had during the healing service would remain with her and be deepened. This gift of faith in a personal, loving God as our Father is basic to all healing. Brenda cried, I suppose, because she did not know what was happening inside her. It was something she secretly longed for but could not express in words. That it should happen to her was so wonderful and unexpected that the tears began to flow like living water washing away her fears. In a true sense she was baptised in the Spirit.

She needed healing of memories, her false sense of guilt and a thousand and one other things from her past which robbed her of the joy of living. Even though it took over a year for Brenda to be healed of her deep-seated lack of joy, today she is a new person, not complete yet because her healing process, like that for us all, will continue throughout her life. She needed not so much to be healed of fear, but of her fear of healing. This healing, I believe, can only come from God. Time and again Jesus told his followers, 'Fear not, little flock' (Luke 12:32) because God is our Father and we have to trust him with our lives (see Luke 12:22–31). This putting aside of fear, and learning to trust, happens deep inside us as persons where God alone reaches and makes us whole. Without the gift then no further healing can take place. Once we know God loves us then we can come out of darkness into light and learn to love God and other people. Our lives will take on the colour of hope and joy.

The fear which destroys our relationship with God, our neighbour and within ourselves drains us of hope and joy. Fear-filled people, like Brenda used to be, are prophets of doom and gloom whose outlook for the future is pessimistic. They look on their world 'darkly' and are unwilling or unable to take a risk on anything. Afraid of the world, they live at a 'low level' bordering on depression. In our healing services I have encountered many people who are so devoid of hope that it is extremely difficult to minister to them. They do not believe that God loves them, or wants anything better for them, and so for them there is no expectancy, no hope of healing. They have a basic lack of faith in a God who loves them as a Father.

George is typical of many people with this mentality. He does not accept or believe in healing because of his lack of hope. He is a cynic. He trusts no one, not even himself, and is not surprised or shocked when he hears of people's weaknesses or downfalls. He seems to relish it and takes great pleasure in bad news. He walks with measured tread and stooped shoulders as if the sky were about to fall on him, or the earth swallow him up. A few minutes in his company makes you aware of how negative and distrustful he is of people. 'We live in a wicked world,' he told me time and again, 'and everyone is tarred with the same brush of sin. I think hope is a grand illusion that things will get better, whereas in fact they can only get worse. I'm glad I'm not a young man today with my whole life before me. Things have got worse in my lifetime, and I have no reason to expect that they will get better in the years ahead.' Trying to encourage George to be hopeful is like giving the kiss of life to a corpse. He came to just one healing service and never returned. Even though he saw people being healed and restored around him, he refused to believe that it was anything other than a temporary 'healing' which would not last. For George, unlike Brenda, there is as yet no happy ending.

Hope is the spiritual dimension so lacking, not only in our world, but also in our churches. The Christian community that does not preach joy and hope in and out of season is not being true to the gospel of Jesus Christ. We are meant to hope not only for the joy of heaven, but also to live a meaningful, joyful life on earth. The lack of hope among many people who are regular church-goers is a phenomenon of the healing ministry which has deeply saddened me. Our congregations, instead of being conscious of God's love for them, are often overwhelmed by a sense of sin and their own personal guilt. The false teaching on the nature of God which does not portray him as a loving Father whom they have personally experienced, has done untold harm. It is something which, in terms of inner healing, is extremely difficult to eradicate. Such people need 'de-briefing'. This teaching, begun in childhood years and fostered in the family environment, is unchristian and crippling of the individual's human personality.

Many a Christian is constantly being told that his only hope is to do penance for his sins, and he *might* get to heaven. In himself he is not worth very much, and left to his own devices he would soon bring shame on himself, his family and his church. This teaching is totally alien to the gospel and leaves its victims bereft of hope or any confidence in God or themselves. If people are saddled with this insupportable burden of unworthiness and personal guilt which destroys hope, then how can they be expected to look on life as something joyful and precious. They are like drowning people who would soon pull us down to their level of joyless living if we did not come up for air with which to fill our being.

While faith means that we believe in a personal loving God, hope makes us aware that God believes in us. He trusts us and for this reason he gives us freedom as our special gift. Because he trusts us we need to learn to trust, to believe, in ourselves. We are, each one of us, special people. This is what Brenda believes today. It is the source of her joy and fulfilment in life. At the age of fifty-three, she has discovered that life is worth living. She has begun to live.

Most people who come to us for inner healing are in great need of hope. Many, like George, do not expect to be healed because of the mythical monstrous God on which they have been reared! As a young boy I had a deep fear of God in my life, because of false teaching at school, and I have first-hand experience of what it has done to damage and limit me in my approach to life. This fear persisted long after I became a priest, but it has helped me to understand the emptiness and fear of people who think that their healing is impossible. Uncontrolled fear binds us in the entangling bonds of self-depreciation. It will not let us be free to be ourselves, to be joyful and, therefore, to enjoy life. It holds us captive so that we never come to appreciate who we really are or realise our potential. This captivity and deprivation is typified for me in the story of an eaglet that was stolen from its nest by a young man who, having bound its wings, put it among some chickens scratching for food in the farmyard. One day an eagle soared majestically over the farm, and the young eagle, looking up, said, 'How I wish I could fly like that.' 'Don't be silly,' said one of the chickens, 'that is the eagle, the king of birds. You're not like him. You are just an ordinary chicken like us.' So the young eagle grew up and died, never knowing who he was, or that he was born destined to fly. There are many bound eagles in our world, who have lost their hope of flying and being free to spread their wings. The bound eagle, and nature itself, is the poorer for its captivity because it will never experience the joy of flying with wings outstretched. Nor will we see the beauty of God in the serene power of one of his creatures as it majestically uses its wings to hover and fly, more graceful than the most perfect ballet dancer.

Christian hope tells me that I am one of God's eagles, and that I am gloriously free to be myself. We were meant to be free and fully human, and to live the kind of life that God wants us to live. We are set free by the truth of Christ's saving gospel that we are children of a Father who loves us even when we find it difficult to see any reasons for loving ourselves. He wants us to enjoy life and to be free as eagles. 'When Christ freed us, he meant us to remain free. Stand firm, therefore, and do not submit again to the yoke of slavery.' (Galatians 5:1) We will enjoy

the glorious liberty of the children of God, for that is who
we really are. We must never allow anyone to take our
heritage away from us. Fearful people, afraid of being
happy, are prisoners in a cage of their own making. They
will not give the key to anyone or use it themselves. 'The
glory of God is man fully alive' says St Irenaeus. Yet most
of us live at a tenth of our potential. We are like an
iceberg with only a tenth of ourselves above the surface.
So many people go through life without ever having really
lived. What a tragedy it is that we Christians are not filled
with the joy of living. We do not say a full 'Yes' to life but
surround our reply with 'maybe' or 'if only' or 'perhaps'
or some other restricting phrase. We are conditioned
people giving conditioned responses when we were meant
to shout 'Amen, Alleluia' to every moment of our lives in
God's creation on earth. I like to think that God loves
the sound of laughter which comes from the heart and
lifts the spirit.

If we live in hope then we will trust that God will help
us to overcome the barriers which separate us from loving
our true selves and enjoying life. Life will become an
exciting challenge. We will come constantly to new and
exciting discoveries of what hidden and wonderful depths
there are within us, and in the world around us, once we
have uncontrolled fear behind us. As a Christian, I believe
that we cannot perform this task alone. Christ discovers
within and with us our new joyful self, so that we begin
to live a new life: 'For anyone who is in Christ, there is a
new creation; the old creation has gone, and now the new
one is here. It is all God's work. It was God who reconciled
us to himself through Christ' (2 Corinthians 5:17–18).
The more fully we accept ourselves, the more successfully
we can allow and want ourselves to be changed for the
better and to be happy.

Change is a slow and often painful process and, therefore, we must be patient with ourselves. 'We groan and
find it a burden being still in this tent, not that we want

to strip if off, but to put the second garment over it and to have what must die taken up into life. This is the purpose for which God made us, and he has given us the pledge of the Spirit.' (2 Corinthians 5:4-5) As hope emerges, then fear will correspondingly disappear. If we really want to be happy then we must be prepared to change. Healing always involves change, and Christian hope gives us the courage to believe that however difficult the process, we will win through. One of the saddest events in my life as a priest is the memory of a person who was an alcoholic. He was aware of what his increasing bouts of drinking were doing to his wife, his family and himself. He felt he could never change. Haunted by fear, he took his own life in a moment of despondency. He had lost all sense of hope. He forgot to concentrate on his love for his family and their love for him. In a sense, if we really thought we could never change we would be guilty of spiritual suicide.

People without hope are frightened of life and of change. They see healing as threatening their pattern of life. Yet no one can be healed unless he is prepared to change and be changed. Whenever I encounter such joy-less people in a healing session I feel their subconscious hopelessness, even their hostility. I hear the tears they shed inside and know that they cannot express in words their deepest feelings. Their healing, while difficult, is often the most profound. Ken is typical of the kind of person I mean. His story is very like that of Brenda.

'Ever since I was a young boy I had it drilled into me by my parents, teachers and everyone else, that the most important virtue was humility. I was never to think well of myself – in fact, the opposite. I began to believe that without the practice of my religion I would degenerate into the sinful monster I knew I was inside. I went to church out of fear, and clung on religiously to everything my parents held dear, especially after they died. If I did anything else, I felt I was being disloyal to them. I felt that if there was a hell, then if left to myself, that is where I was going. Married, and with a family, I treated my children in the same way that my parents treated me. When my children left home, and the practice of their religion, I cut them off. I felt betrayed. One day – why, I don't know – I came to one of your healing sessions. You spoke of God's love for each one of us, and how important it was for us to be hopeful. I scoffed at your teaching this 'new' religion, but when I looked round at the congregation I knew they were praying in a way which was different from our normal Sunday service because they really believed. When you came to my pew and asked if you could pray over me, I turned you down and looked at you with as much hostility as I could muster. You passed on and I had mixed feelings of relief and rejection. At the end of the service everyone was happy except me. I felt that it was like Christmas Day and I didn't belong with these people! I couldn't help but notice their joy, not over-the-top as I expected, and it accentuated my own emptiness, despair and lack of hope.'

Ken came, reluctantly at first, many times to our healing services but his rehabilitation, like that of Brenda, took a long time. It is still going on and the change in his life is quite remarkable. He is becoming a new person. His attitude towards his parents, his wife and his children had to be healed, and there are even yet some sore and stressful areas into which he finds it hard to enter. He had, as is necessary in such cases, to unlearn a lot of false teaching. In our El Shaddai ministry of inner healing we pray constantly for the Kens, Brendas and Georges of this world, that sometime in their lives they will discover who, and how precious, they are and why they are uniquely different in God the Father's loving creation. Each person is special to him. In God's eyes none of us is a faceless, hopeless person. *Our happiness is of paramount importance to him.* He trusts us with life and believes in our desire to be open to him and to be truly happy in ourselves.

There was a Ken in me. Like Ken, I only began to hope and to be joyful deep within myself when I began to believe that God trusted me. I realised then that I was lovable in myself. This is the great value of hope. It makes me aware that God wants me as his partner and friend. He wants me to share my life with him just as in Christ he shares his life with me. God is unique and so am I. What makes me different from everyone else is not my fingerprints, but the still centre of my being, round which my whole personality revolves. It is there that I shall find inner peace and the secret of the joy of living. Yet that was where for years I was afraid to go because of the shallowness of my faith and hope. It is where God dwells within me, and the devil did not want me to find it, because then I would have found a power within myself which would destroy my fear. I would discover I was an eagle who was born to fly.

One of the greatest healings people can receive is to be encouraged to hope that their lives will change, especially when things go wrong for them and they see no way out of the tragedy which is dragging them down. This is a time when those nearest and dearest to us need to hold us up lest we sink into the depths of despair which is self-destructive and a recipe for disaster.

David is a typical example of the power of hope which lifts up our spirits when things go wrong in our lives. He had a very happy family life and a job which, though demanding, gave him a sense of fulfilment. He was a generous, caring, joyful person. Then things went dramatically wrong. His firm was taken over by a French company and it was obvious that his services were no longer required. Pressure was put on him to such an extent that he had no option but to resign. This he did in a flurry of anger and bitterness. For a while he felt great, because he had the courage to tell his boss what he thought of him. But the euphoria did not last long. David became resentful of what happened to him. His whole life-style changed. He tried various jobs with little success. He was so edgy with his wife that their marriage began to disintegrate. He went to church but could not pray. He was in a cloud of despair. When he was at his lowest ebb the tide turned. This is how he described what happened.

'I could not believe what was happening to me. I just could not take it on board. I began to discover sides to me which I hated and I started to hate myself and drew in on myself. At first I prayed but soon I became very angry with God. Why me? What had I done wrong? Then I realised for the first time in my life that I could not manage my life on my own. I needed my wife and family. I needed God. My life returned but, my goodness, it was a slow process. I started to trust God with my life. Every other avenue seemed to be closed to me. I had good days and bad days. I had to come to terms with the 'not so nice' side of the kind of person I was. I accepted myself, knowing that God loved me and wanted what was best for me. My hope was not misplaced. I realise now that life is not all sunshine, but it is not all darkness either. I have changed. I hope I am joyful but now I know I am a fragile person who needs handling with care. I treat other people more sensitively now that I am discovering my true self. This is the secret of my joy and happiness.'

We all have dark periods in our lives. Like David, I too needed hope in my time of crisis, wondering where was the God who loved me and when, if ever, he was going to heal me. In hindsight, I see it now as a very special time. It was a desert experience which prepared me for my inner healing ministry and for much of what is of lasting value in my life. Because I lived so long in the twilight and experienced so much spiritual dryness in my life, I was able to approach the healing ministry in what, I hope, is a *compassion* born of experience. That is why the main thrust of our El Shaddai ministry is to stress that in order to enjoy life and look forward with joy to the future, we need to believe in God's love, never-failing for us however dark the situation is, otherwise we will find it impossible to hope. If we are filled with fear and foreboding, we will block out of our minds and hearts the merciful forgiveness of God our loving Father, and concentrate on his justice and righteous anger, of which we are the victims. While we allow that the story of the Prodigal Son may be authentic for others, we still see ourselves as the son who never returned home, never quite made it. This lack of trust in God's forgiveness is fuelled by those who, in order to keep us 'under control', over-stress God's scrupulous justice. What they really mean is not justice but law. Those who insisted on the letter of the law got short shrift from Jesus. He sat lightly to laws which ignored the need to love the person and to enhance his quality of life. Mercy and justice for me are as one in the person of God the Father and I would rather know his justice than the mercy of the most merciful person in the world.

In our healing sessions we find time and again this exaggerated and false emphasis on God's justice, overshadowing and blighting the hope and joy in the lives of so many otherwise beautiful people. God's justice, so often misunderstood and preached as the measure of God's unremitting adherence to the letter of the law, fills many people with irrational fear. Yet the one commandment necessary for happiness, that we should 'love God with all our heart, and our neighbour as ourselves', is often passed over lightly or even ignored. God's justice should mean freedom, not tyranny or slavery. Justice in our Father's eyes is reflected in his attitude to the Prodigal Son, and that of Jesus to the woman taken in adultery. God's mercy always seasons his justice. People long to be free as eagles but are afraid to stretch out their wings. They do not dare to hope because basically they do not believe in Christ's resurrection and his triumph over sin. They do not really believe that they are forgiven and so guilt binds their wings and prevents them from being free. They do not claim the victory because they think the battle is still on and they are on the losing side. So since the quest for self-discovery, self-appreciation and the joy of living requires hope, they call off the search because they find no reason within themselves for hoping, no cause for being joyful. They do not return to their Father's house because of what they think his treatment of them will be. They put the Father's unchanging love for them out of their minds; happiness is for others but not for them. Yet we have no need to be afraid of what we may find deep within ourselves. Whatever it is, and however repulsive it may seem to us, it is already redeemed. The person without hope is unforgiving of others but especially of himself. Yet unless we forgive ourselves then how can we pray the Lord's Prayer, 'Forgive us our trespasses as we forgive those who trespass against us'? If we are not merciful with ourselves, then we will mete out justice and vengeance to other people.

We have experienced God's forgiveness, and so we must 'forgive each other as readily as God forgave you in Christ' (Ephesians 4:32). We have no need to be afraid of God our Father. In the knowledge that we are damaged people who have been healed, and are being healed, by God's love, we can then go out to others in gratitude and mercy. We too often look on this phrase of the Lord's Prayer – 'Forgive us as we forgive others' – as if we are appealing to God's justice instead of his mercy. 'If justice were our plea,' Portia said to Shylock, 'then none of us would see salvation.' God's mercy is our reason for hoping.

The knowledge of God's mercy to us not only destroys our fear and gives us a truer appreciation of our own worth, but it also opens up his healing grace to others through us and we become instruments of his peace, forgiveness and hope. If we do not preach and live by hope then we will soon forget that God is merciful and forgives our weaknesses. In a human family the one who causes the most mischief and worry is often the most loved. So it is with us and God. He does not love us because we are clean and shining like Little Lord Fauntleroys, but because we are being ourselves as he made us. We are happy to be in his presence playing like children who are often up to mischief. 'And if we are children, we are heirs as well: heirs of God and coheirs with Christ, sharing his sufferings so as to share his glory.' (Romans 8:17) St Paul reminds us: 'You are God's chosen race, his saints; he loves you' (Colossians 3:12). This doctrine of God's forgiving love is most difficult to get across to fearful people. Once they believe it then fear will dissolve like ice before the noonday sun and they will become hope-filled, joyful people who will fly like eagles.

Fearful people have little joy or hope in their lives because they have a low appreciation of themselves which is at the root of their fear. Even though they believe that God loves them they are still so conscious of their own sinfulness that they do not believe in *their own value*. In fact, God's love and our sinfulness are seen as contradictory and irreconcilable. In such cases we need to convince ourselves that 'by turning everything to their good, God co-operates with all those who love him' (Romans 8:28). St Paul was convinced of the power of Christ: 'There is nothing I cannot master with the help of the One who gives me strength.' (Philippians 4:13) The Bible is full of images that inspire confidence in the love of God the Father for his children. 'Do not take fright. Yahweh your God goes in front of you and will be fighting on your side as you saw him fight for you in Egypt. In the wilderness too, you saw him: how Yahweh carried you, as a man carries his child, all along the road you travelled on the way to this place.' (Deuteronomy 1:30–31)

If we want to experience the personal love of God our Father and be filled with hope and joy in our lives then we all need to be released by the Spirit of the risen Jesus so that we can come out of the dungeon of controlling fear. Christ has come, as Isaiah foretold, to preach liberty to captives. The prison bars of self cannot contain our spirit of freedom. The resurrection of the Lord has set us free. It is his Spirit that is changing us by giving us hope and making us come more fully alive and joyful. 'Now this Lord is the Spirit, and where the Spirit of the Lord is, there is freedom. And we, with our unveiled faces reflecting like mirrors the brightness of the Lord, all grow brighter and brighter as we are turned into the image that we reflect; this is the work of the Lord who is Spirit.' (2 Corinthians 3:18) It is by rising above our false self, which is often rooted in fear and an overwhelming sense of our own unworthiness, that we allow the inner true self to emerge into the light. We will then begin to live more fully, and in love to find true happiness and inner peace. We become a people of hope and joy.

Hope teaches us to evaluate ourselves correctly and gives us the courage to continue our search for self-discovery, self-fulfilment and the joy of living. Without hope we would soon abandon the search and settle for second best. Faith and hope are both needed in our struggle with fear. Faith gives us, as it were, insights into God, and and hope insights into ourselves. The authentic self tends to show itself in moments of strong emotions of joy or sorrow – moments when the very existence and nature of God is challenged, as well as our own capacity to see the situation through. The devil attacks us on both fronts of faith and hope: he inhibits us. The dictionary defines 'to inhibit' as 'to restrain' or 'to hinder'. Martin Buber calls the devil 'the hinderer', the evil influence that works through our feelings of fear, doubt and discouragement to prevent us from seeing who and what we are and what our life is all about. The devil likes us to remain displaced persons who are lost without hope of ever finding ourselves and our destiny. He is the great destroyer of true self-love. He does not want us to fly and he tells us that we never can and we never will. He destroys our confidence in life and in ourselves. We feel despair instead of hope, sadness rather than joy.

If we abandon our search for a purpose to our lives, or despair of ever being the kind of person God wants us to be, then fear will regain control of our lives because fear is basically a lack of faith and hope. We will not believe that God has the power to help us in our lives, and even if we did, we think that he does not care anyway because he does not really believe in us. We reason that since we got ourselves into the mess in which we find ourselves, then we will be left on our own to get ourselves out of it. What an insult to God! Many of us are hung up on our approach to God and to life. We try to find personal fulfilment by our own efforts alone and feel so let down when we fail that we give up hope and are less prepared to try again, until eventually we give up altogether. To go it alone in our search for a purpose in life and true happiness is an impossible task. St Paul reminds us that only God can make our hidden selves flourish so that our lives become more whole, hopeful and joyful.

> Out of his infinite glory, may he give you the power through his Spirit for your hidden self to grow strong, so that Christ may live in your hearts through faith, and then, planted in love and built on love, you will, with all the saints have strength to grasp the breadth and length, the height and depth; until, knowing the love of Christ, which is beyond all knowledge, you are filled with the utter fullness of God. Glory be to him whose power, working in us, can do infinitely more than we can ask or imagine, glory be to him from generation to generation in the Church and in Christ Jesus for ever and ever. Amen.' (Ephesians 3:16–21)

God does not want us to face all the problems of life alone. He is with us in all things, sustaining us and helping us. We have to trust God with our lives as a friend who will never fail us. The whole purpose of hope is to foster in us this attitude of mind so necessary for peace and joy in our lives.

Hope reminds us that God cares for the individual as someone unique whom he loves. 'I have branded you on the palms of my hands' (Isaiah 49:16). He calls us by name out of the darkness into the light of his life. 'Do not be afraid, for I have redeemed you, I have called you by your name, you are mine.' (Isaiah 43:1) Each one of us is infinitely precious to him. We may be expendable to institutions, but God is not an institution. Institutions come and go but God's love is enduring. He is a Father who loves us and goes on loving us whether we acknowledge it or not. The Lord assures us: 'Can you not buy two sparrows for a penny? And yet not one falls to the ground without your Father knowing. Why, every hair on your head has been counted. So there is no need to be afraid; you are worth more than hundreds of sparrows.' (Matthew 10:29–31)

We trust ourselves and our hidden selves in faith to the God whom we have never seen, and whom we only know by faith as our loving Father. Faith and hope give us courage to face up to all the challenges of life and to the weaknesses we discover in ourselves. What is courage but the power of life to affirm itself against all the odds? It is a positive refusal to be overcome. Jesus calls us friends and, therefore, is someone who shares his life with us. 'I have told you all this so that you may find peace in me. In the world you will have trouble, but be brave: I have conquered the world.' (John 16:33) He and I are an absolute majority in any situation. We believe in his words. If we really believe that we are loved and watched over by a Father who sent his Son to be with us always then why should we fear?

People of hope live one day at a time, remembering Christ's words that 'each day has enough troubles of its own' (Matthew 6:34). We change every day through Christ's power working in us. We Christians are people of the 'now'. What we do not achieve in this life God will bring to perfection in the next. So we are not to worry unduly about our apparently slow progress in our journey back to the Father. Some days we can manage a good day's journey; other days it will not be so good. However, we are pilgrims and so long as we keep our sights on Christ we will not go far wrong. Christ is our friend and guide! In his company we journey through life in hope and joy.

9

Afraid to Speak Out

There is a time for keeping silent, a time for speaking (Ecclesiastes 3:7). Silence is not always golden. If we really want to be true to ourselves and retain our inner peace, then there will be occasions when we have to speak out. We would rather be without the pain it causes others or the hurt we suffer ourselves, yet it would be wrong for us to remain silent. We have to stand up and be counted on behalf of those principles which we hold dear as an essential part of us. We know deep down in our heart that this is the only way we can be true to ourselves and our conscience. When we remain silent, even though we may delude ourselves in the short term, eventually we lose respect for ourselves in our own eyes. If we do this often enough then, eventually, conscience will give up the struggle and remain silent because it has been gagged by uncontrolled fear which has compromised us and eroded our value as persons. Fear has become our master and we become non-persons, ciphers in a controlled system. Speaking up for truth on behalf of others has its own price; it costs nothing less than everything. There are situations all round the world where, in the face of the most horrendous physical and mental tortures, people of faith have spoken out in order to be true to the Christian gospel. Jesus said to his disciples, 'To you my friends I say: Do not be afraid of those who kill the body and after that can do no more. I will tell you whom to fear: fear him who, after he has killed, has the power to cast into hell.' (Luke 12:4–5)

Why are we afraid to be true to ourselves and speak out? Are we people who want peace at any price? Is it because we want to curry favour with people of power and influence so that our own power position is not put in jeopardy? Is it more important for us to be one of the crowd rather than raise a dissenting voice? Do we rationalise our silence by pretending that our inter-vention would be of no consequence to the final out-come? Do we try to convince ourselves that it is better to be silent now so that later on either the problem will resolve itself or we might find a better opportunity to speak up? Silence can be golden and is a very powerful healing medium, but when it is bred by uncontrolled fear, then it destroys the individual at every level. We will never stand up and be counted unless and until we control fear so that we can be true to ourselves and be false to no one.

When we are afraid to stand up for those values which are essential to our own lives and those of our neighbours, then we become diminished as persons. As a conse-quence, we are less human, less Christian. We have failed not only ourselves, but damaged our relationship with our neighbour and with God our Father. We have silenced the still, small *voice of conscience* and are less likely to listen to it in the future. Silence born out of exaggerated fear condemns us. We forget that evil triumphs when good people do or say nothing when they should. The silence of betrayal is one of the greatest evils which affects our fallen human nature. We choose to remain silent because of fear which controls our spirit. We have not the moral courage to do or say the things we know deep down in our hearts we should. Intimidated by people and situ-ations, we shrink as persons by our silence. We are dam-aged and soiled by guilty silence. We are all guilty in varying degrees of the betrayal of our consciences. We do or say things which are alien to us as persons and as Christians, fearing the consequences to ourselves which speaking out involves. We turn a blind eye to the harsh treatment meted out unjustly to others because of our silence. We do not want to get involved.

It is the story of the Good Samaritan all over again. Selfishly, we ask ourselves the question: 'What will happen *to me* if I take a stand on this issue? What will happen to my image, my job, my security, my future?' If I am a Christian, then I should reverse the question in my concern for others. 'What will happen to others if I don't make a stand?' My Christian duty is to do and say what Jesus would do or say in my situation, and not be over-concerned with my image or what others think of me. Because I have to live with myself, then if I am a Christian I have to remind myself constantly that God is my Father; he will protect my life and my future if I have faith and trust in him. As I have grown older I have realised more and more that even though other people may choose to remain silent, if I know deep within me that this is not the course I can follow, then I have no other option but to speak out. No one will buy my unchristian silence; I cannot allow anyone or any institution to silence me and diminish me as a person. I have a right and a duty to myself and to others to speak out because it is part of me as a person if I want to live at peace with myself.

All my life I have seen the distress and consequences of wrongful silence and the feeling of betrayal which it causes in all sections of society. I have been down that road myself. It concerned, especially, my involvement with the Peace Movement in Northern Ireland in 1976. I spoke out for peace and hoped that many other priests would follow my example. I committed myself to its cause, and looked for support and encouragement from my Church. There was little or none. On the contrary, I was side-lined and left to walk more or less alone. I became a non-person for six years, without any diocesan assignment or acknowledgement of my very demanding and sensitive role as a peace-maker. It taught me that being true to conscience tests every fibre of your emotional and spiritual being. It is the killing fields of cowards.

In the consequent wilderness experience I went through the whole gamut of emotions. I felt at times confused, angry, frustrated, rejected, even bitter. The journey back to wholeness and acceptance of my own weakness and that of others was a long one. I needed healing. I believed when I supported the Peace People of Northern Ireland that I could not do anything else if I wanted to live at peace with myself and my Christian conscience. I hoped I was doing what God wanted me to do, because no matter what anyone said or did, I had to be God's man. Many Job's comforters came offering me advice, but living in the wilderness with time to think, I was able to place institutions and people in their proper place on the rungs of the ladder of my life. They became low down and gradually faded away into the periphery of my life. God my Father became the supreme absolute for me. His love for me changed my life and taught me to love myself as I should. Everything else was secondary and of relatively less importance. Even though it was excruciatingly painful at the time, I am glad I walked in the valley of darkness. In that journey in which I found myself, I was spiritually healed of seeking human approval and respect for anything I would ever achieve in my life; these worldly values and approval are but straws in the wind. I hope in the process that I have learned the destructiveness of resentment and the danger of negative silence by which others are hurt and their faith diluted. Because I was hurt by guilty silence and healed, I believe that I am now better equipped to help those who suffer the same trauma. God's ways are certainly not ours and it is he alone who heals us. We have to go on believing in the dark days that there is a purpose in our suffering even though, at the time, it is hidden from our eyes. This is for us a growing time as persons, with all the pain involved.

Was I wrong to commit myself and foolish to speak out in the cause of peace in Northern Ireland? Was it the right time? I don't know, and perhaps I never shall, but I still really believe that, as Christians, we will be given the right time and the right words to speak, which will be true and healing. Jesus promised us: 'And when they lead you away to hand you over, do not worry beforehand about what to say; no, say whatever is given to you when the time comes, because it is not you who will be speaking: it will be the Holy Spirit.' (Mark 13:11)

In our dilemma as to whether it is best to remain silent or speak out, we turn to the life of Jesus himself. Jesus experienced the terrible consequences of cowardly silence in his own life. Silence is often cowardly and destructive. It was the silence of those who should have spoken out which resulted in his crucifixion. Their silence was wrong. Jesus, himself, was aware of the consequences of speaking out so he himself had to be on his guard against the rabbis and the Pharisees. He was a threat to their power, especially because of his healing, his teaching and his popularity. They were jealous of him. In the beginning of his public ministry he counselled his followers and he himself practised a silence born of wisdom. He maintained a low profile because he discerned clearly that the people of power round him were fearful of change or anything which would threaten their power base. He made a balanced judgement on when and how to act.

The worst enemies of people who want the power to be in control of others are those who are not afraid to speak up against a system which they believe is destructive of people's freedom to grow in inner peace and fulfilment. Jesus was such a person. The first time he spoke publicly was in his own village of Nazara.

He came to Nazara, where he had been brought up,

and went into the synagogue as he usually did. He stood up to read, and they handed him the scroll of the prophet Isaiah. Unrolling the scroll, he found the place where it said:

The Spirit of the Lord has been given to me, for he has anointed me. He has sent me to bring the good news to the poor, to proclaim liberty to captives and to the blind new sight, to set the downtrodden free, to proclaim the Lord's year of favour.

He then rolled up the scroll, gave it back to the assistant and sat down . . . Then he began to speak to them . . . 'I tell you solemnly, no prophet is ever accepted in his own country . . . In the prophet Elisha's time there were many lepers in Israel, but none of these was cured except the Syrian, Naaman.' When they heard this, everyone in the synagogue was enraged. They sprang to their feet and hustled him out of the town; and they took him to the brow of the hill their town was built on, intending to throw him down the cliff, but he slipped through the crowd and walked away. (Luke 4:16–20, 24, 27–30)

Because the people were not ready to listen to him with an open mind when he spoke of freedom, he had to 'tailor' his message to suit his listeners without comprom-ising it. He was prudent with a prudence born of discern-ment rather than cautious with a caution spawned by power, cowardice or fear. He told people time and again not to speak about his acts of healing because it would be counter-productive to his mission. 'As Jesus went on his way, two blind men followed him shouting, "Take pity on us, Son of David." . . . Then he [Jesus] touched their eyes, saying, "Your faith deserves it, so let this be done for you." And their sight returned. Then Jesus warned them, "Take care that no one learns about this". But when they had gone, they talked about him all over the countryside.' (Matthew 9:27, 29–31)

The Jewish leaders saw the dangers inherent in a situation where the people flocked in their thousands to hear Jesus preach and to beg him to heal them. 'Then the chief priests and Pharisees called a meeting. 'Here is this man [Jesus] working all these signs, they said, and what action are we taking? If we let him go on in this way everybody will believe in him and the Romans will come and destroy the Holy Place and our nation.' (John 11:47–48) The great double-think and the sop to their conscience! They had already planned to crucify Jesus; now they had to devise a crime to fit the punishment. Given the twisted thinking of their leaders, I have often wondered why so few Jews, who were such a religious people, failed to speak up in his defence, when he was put on trial for his life before Pilate. Where were all those whom he had healed, those who had listened to him, convinced that no one spoke with such authority as he did? A passage from St John's Gospel holds the key. 'Though they had been present when he gave so many signs, they did not believe in him . . . And yet there were many who did believe in him, even among the leading men, but they did not admit it, through fear of the Pharisees and fear of being expelled from the synagogue: they put honour from men before the honour that comes from God.' (John 12:37, 42–43) The fault lay in the fact that they looked over their shoulders too anxiously in the direction of their religious leaders in order to gauge their reaction and seek their approval. They were so full of religion that they were lacking in faith, and so they buried their consciences in the treacherous quicksands of conformity. Are we not guilty today of the same fault, afraid to speak up and question those things around us which we know are wrong? False notions of social and religious acceptance rob us of our freedom and courage as individuals. Jesus set us free because he taught by love; systems control us by fear. St Paul reminds us: 'when Christ freed us, he meant us to remain free. Stand firm, therefore, and do not submit again to the yoke of slavery.' (Galatians 5:1)

When the time came for Jesus to speak more publicly, there was no mistaking his message.

> The scribes and the Pharisees began a furious attack on him [Jesus] and tried to force answers from him on innumerable questions, setting traps to catch him out in something he might say. Meanwhile, the people had gathered in their thousands so that they were treading on one another. And he began to speak, first of all to his disciples. 'Be on your guard against the yeast of the Pharisees – that is, their hypocrisy. Everything that is now covered will be uncovered, and everything now hidden will be made clear. For this reason, whatever you have said in the dark will be heard in the daylight, and what you have whispered in hidden places will be proclaimed on the housetops.' (Luke 11:53–54, 12:1–3)

Jesus threw down the gauntlet to his enemies. From now on for him and his followers silence would no longer be golden.

I know from experiences in my own life that if I want to control my fear of the consequences of speaking out on something which is precious in my life and belief, then because I am a damaged person I have to acknowledge that I shall be tempted to remain silent. I know only too well that I need help from a source higher than human help, and this is what conscience is all about. I need to pray that I shall be given the wisdom to do and accept what is right for me. Jesus acknowledged this during his crisis in the Garden of Gethsemane: 'Father,' he said, 'if you are willing, take this cup away from me' (Luke 22:42). His faith was being built up over the years, and would equip him to deal with his moment of trial. I know that however strong I think my faith is, I am still in need of divine help in each crisis if I am not to fail in witnessing to my Christian belief; I cannot go it alone. St Peter failed his master, and so have I on many occasions in the past. Peter's faith in, and love for, Jesus were his outstanding virtues. Jesus gave him the name Peter, meaning 'rock', because he was to be the model of faith for all Christians everywhere. 'So I now say to you: you are Peter and on this rock [of faith] I will build my Church.' (Matthew 16:18) When Peter was placed in a situation of fear in a courtyard with hostile Roman soldiers, he reacted as a frightened man. His faith and love for his master were being tested in the harsh climate of the cold, chilling blast of hatred far removed from the warm atmosphere of the company of like-minded companions. Even though he was spiritually and emotionally close to Jesus, his enemies were physically nearer.

There have been many times in the past when I too should have spoken up and did not. I rationalised my silence in a thousand and one different ways. I know now that I put myself before the message. Because I wanted to be a survivor I was intent on saving my own skin, even though I would not acknowledge this even to myself at the time. Worldly standards in the worst sense penetrated my thinking and life-style, because I wanted to be part of a system to which I gave unquestioning obedience and loyalty. I was not convinced of the absolute truth of the Christian message and so I compromised. Unknown to myself, my faith and moral outlook were adversely affected. I was afraid to be different from those around me. Thank God, I hope I have put that fear behind me long ago, because I saw the havoc it was doing to my life and inner peace. I yearned to grow as a person and as a Christian. I needed to find and experience the love that would make this possible.

None of us, whether we are Christians or not, will ever stand up in our situation and be counted unless and until we realise that we are important as individuals and that we have a voice. If we really want to be more fully human then we shall not be silent when anyone tries to control us and attempts to take away our peace and freedom to be ourselves. We know that silence in such circumstances is self-destructive. We have a purpose in life, just as Jesus had, given to us by God our Father. He loves us. We are *personal* to him and he called us by name. There can be only one 'me' and, like each individual person, I am unique. Love of ourselves and being free to be true to ourselves is essential for our growth as persons. It is the most precious thing which we guard with life itself. When we are controlled by people and events, then life loses its meaning. We need to remind ourselves constantly that inner peace is Christ's gift to us and no one should be allowed to take it from us. It can be, and is often, taken away by those nearest and dearest to us, who, with all the good will in the world, do not allow us the freedom to grow and be ourselves. Our parents, or our husband or wife can so dominate us that we remain silent for the sake of peace. We do not want to hurt them by speaking out, but in the process of remaining silent we hurt everyone, including ourselves. Our quality of life is diluted.

In the El Shaddai ministry we frequently encounter people whose family situations destroy them as individuals and rob them of their inner peace. Yet the family is where we should grow to maturity as persons. Jesus went to Nazareth with Mary and Joseph and there 'he increased in wisdom, in stature and in favour with God and men' (Luke 2:52). A family which is built on love will always leave everyone free to speak out because what is said is nurtured in a dialogue where each one listens and is seen as an individual. No one, especially parents, has the right to control another to the extent that they do not give them sufficient space to grow and spread their wings. Parents are like eagles who teach their young how to fly. They have the privilege of being in a unique position to their children. We can have only one father and one mother. Their privilege is to love their children, not control them. The controlling influence of parents on children will be love. Parents will encourage their children to grow to be themselves, not a replica of the parents. When children are taken over completely by one or both parents, then someone in the family has to stand up and be counted. It will never be easy, and it certainly was not so in Susan's case. Her father, John, always wanted to be in control of the family. He was an honest person, but his blind spot was his failure to admit his mistakes. In his own eyes he was never wrong. This is what he wrote to me:

'I came to your healing service out of curiosity. I have very strong reservations about healing. I suppose I could be called a sceptic. I always planned my life down to the last detail. I like to have everything worked out; time for my work, my home, my hobbies. I was in control of everything and that was the way I wanted it. I provided well for my family and I expected them, in return, to show their gratitude and respect for me. I saw my children through university and, if there was ever any hiccough in their government grants or studies, I used my influence to put things right. Eventually, when they left home to make a life of their own I saw little of them. They made their usual Christmas visit, and remembered my birthday.

'I suspected that there was something missing. I discovered only recently what it might be. That was when I came to your healing service. Mind you, I didn't think I needed healing. You called up whole families to the altar and you said how important it was for the parents to show love for their children. That was the only control they needed. You anointed their hands and then told them to lay their hands in blessing on their children every evening. I was near the front so I could see the look on their faces. I suppose I envied them. Many of them were not rich, but they were happy. They seemed to have something which I hadn't, but then I had something they hadn't. I left the service rather shaken, but I soon regained my composure.

'Next time I met my eldest daughter, Susan, I told her

about the service. She didn't say anything at first, but when I pressed her about my role in her life, and the rest of the family, her answer set me back on my heels. "You were always a good father, a good provider, but you never really told us you loved us or that you needed us. You wanted to be in control and, to be honest, we all thought it was rather frightening. You made everything revolve round you, but didn't you realise how awesome it was? We were never free to be ourselves or to do things for ourselves even if we didn't get them right. We were afraid of you. We respected you, but there was little joy in our relationship with you because you couldn't cope with our growing up. You never sat down with me and asked me what I really wanted. It was always what you wanted for me. Don't think I'm ungrateful, but there was something wrong at home. You always said we were a family, but everything was so controlled that I was sad inside because deep in my heart, I wanted things to be different. It makes me feel awful talking like this to you, but I'm glad you gave me the chance. I hope things will change now, even though it is a bit late." '

John came again to a healing service. This time he was more determined. He didn't want to observe, but to tell me how wrong and how ungrateful his daughter Susan was. He spoke individually to the rest of the family and they all disagreed with Susan. They said he was a good father who provided so well for them. When I suggested that perhaps they were giving him the answers he expected, he would have none of it. I spoke privately to two of his family and they admitted that they did not tell him the truth because it would hurt him and that he wouldn't change anyway. Deep down in their hearts they feared him. I never saw John again.

By far the largest proportion of people who come to us for Christian healing have been damaged as persons by their family background. We pray that those who are emotionally and spiritually damaged may be given the discernment and courage to speak out in love and honesty not only for themselves, but for all those who are emotionally and spiritually damaged, so that with sensitivity and patience they may be shown the right action to take and to follow it through. We all need discernment in our family setting so that we may evaluate ourselves and our relation to other people and situations in a Christian way.

The story of Ellen and Jim and their four children, aged 17, 14, 12 and 10, shows how powerfully the Spirit of God heals his people in a family situation. Jim had a drink problem. He was very violent towards his wife and children whenever he had taken a drink. Both the parents and the children suffered grievously and as a result of this they had become the victims of depression, attempted suicide, asthma, and inability to cope at work and to make friends. In fact Jim was destroying their lives as well as his own by his uncontrollable behaviour. He himself came from a violent family background and he was passing this on to his children. Ellen was, by nature, a timid person; her motto was 'peace at any price'. She had it drilled into her that since she made her own bed she must lie in it. She saw herself as the peacemaker, whereas, in fact, there was chaos all around her. She came to me as a last resort when her eldest son and his father had had such a violent argument that she was afraid it would soon end in tragedy.

Ellen looked such a broken person that my heart went out to her. The first thing I did was to pray with her for her inner peace since without that there could be no progress. She had to learn to love and value herself as a person. It was very painful for her as there were times when she was filled with guilt born out of fear that she was being disloyal to her husband. She felt that these things were better 'kept in the family'. What a false attitude! It was nothing short of incubating violence and destruction in the home. A few months and healing sessions later, she was able to talk more freely about the state of affairs in her family. I told her that I discerned that nothing could be done unless she could bring her husband to talk with me so that I could pray with him. At first he disagreed quite violently. 'There is nothing wrong with me, or the children,' he said. 'All families have their private quarrels.' Violence was all he had ever known; it was a way of life for him. When Ellen came to see me again, she was completely broken in spirit and was prepared to throw in the towel, since she saw no way out of her hopeless situation. I prayed with her that she would regain the inner peace which she had received the last time we prayed together. God was kind to her and her healing was beautiful to witness. Her face lost its beaten look and she was serene and at peace as she rested in the Spirit. I told her to pray for discernment of the Spirit so that she would know when the right time came for her to stand up and be counted for the Christian love and peace which she wanted for herself, her husband and her family. He would put the words on her lips which would touch the mind and heart of her husband, whom she still loved in spite of his violence and excessive drinking. She knew that she owed it to herself and her children not to be silent any longer.

A few weeks later a favourable situation presented itself when there was calm after another violent storm in the family. Courageously and peacefully Ellen told Jim that if his violence and drinking did not stop, she and the children would have to leave home. Instead of the terrible scene she anticipated, he took it quietly. This was, I believe, a minor miracle. The healing of the family had begun. Jim came with Ellen to a healing service where, I think, he expected to be told off by the priest. I felt so sorry for him. Here was no villain, but a very sad and unhappy person who was brutalised by life. He was a greater victim of fear than his wife. He had been deprived by his parents of his right to grow as a person. He was a caged, controlled man who had never tried to understand

and love himself. He was bewildered by what I said to him about the need to love himself and to be at inner peace within himself. No priest had every told him before in a one-to-one situation that he was of great value in himself.

I asked Ellen to tell Jim what was happening to herself and their children. She explained in such a beautiful, tender way how much they all really loved and needed him, that I felt privileged to be there with them both. It was a deeply healing experience for me. He sobbed gently and said how sorry he was, but he just couldn't help himself. I told him that of course he couldn't if left to himself and that he needed to forgive himself. I reminded him that he was not alone with his problem, and that God, his Father, loved him and wanted him to be a whole person and at peace but that it would take time. After a few more services to which they both came, it was obvious that his healing was growing. By now he admitted, both to himself and his wife, his dependence on drink and he joined Alcoholics Anonymous.

The Spirit was at work in Jim's life and his faith became alive. He no longer saw going to church as a duty; it was a part of him which he valued deeply. He was a changed person. Ellen's love for him was a great support. Whenever he felt he would not be able to control his desire for drink, they prayed together for strength. His children changed too. Ellen and Jim shared with them in a much more open way, giving them space to be themselves and to look wider than the family surroundings. They are not completely healed yet of all the hurts they suffered at such a critical and impressionable period in their lives. They had to grow out of their hurtful family situation and the pace of change was not the same for each of them. Strange, but it was the eldest boy of seventeen who was the most supportive and understanding. He was a tower of strength to his parents, his younger brother and his two sisters.

This story of wonderful Christian healing has repeated

itself time and again in hundreds of other cases of family unhappiness when someone has the courage to stand up and be counted. We at El Shaddai have been privileged to be witnesses to it. We encourage people in such destructive family situations to believe that:

- No family situation is outside God's healing love. He is the Father of every family.
- Every member of the family has a right to a peaceful and happy home in which they grow more human, alive and Christian.
- We are all damaged persons, probably none more so than the one who is seen as the disruptive influence in the family.
- We have to stand up and be counted when anyone or any situation in the family threatens its peace.
- The Spirit will give the discernment necessary for the timing and the words necessary for the one who takes the initiative and tries to heal the situation.
- We need to forgive one another in Christian love and realise that healing is a family action in which everyone participates and shares.
- We must use all positive methods which will help create a healing situation, such as counselling, etc.

There are many differences in the two stories which highlight for me the truth that every family is as unique as the individual person. The situations may be similar but never identical. I cannot conclude that in future cases someone like Jim would accept his failing and resolve to change while someone like John would not. I believe, however, that the preparation by Ellen helped to move her husband towards a resolution to alter his style of life. She prayed deeply and, even though encouraged by the healing services to which she came alone, she felt sorely tempted to give up the struggle. Her faith in God the Father's power kept her going, even when she walked in the valley of darkness and despair. She was supported by her children, especially her eldest son. Despite the violence there were strong elements of a family bond between them. They helped each other to create a new situation in which they were able gradually to begin a new life together.

John was a different character from Jim. I perceived him as being self-righteous and judgemental with a consequently closed mind. He came to a healing service to observe and not to pray. He rated himself highly as a father because he was a good provider and seemed to bring up his children with the same set of values. Instead of looking honestly at himself, he looked for reasons to justify himself and prove Susan to be an ungrateful daughter. Knowing both family situations, I would say that John's children are ultimately the more damaged because they carry within themselves the hidden scars of a false sense of materialistic values encouraged in them by their father. I fear that they in their turn will damage their children in a similar way. It is very much a case of the sins of the parents being visited on the children.

Ellen and Susan had the courage to speak up for what, in conscience, they believed to be true and important. The lack of family support for Susan played a considerable part in the final outcome. She should not feel guilty about the reluctance on her father's part to change his life-style and outlook. When we have done all we can, then we have to leave everything else to the Lord. We are not to feel guilty or think that we have not done enough. Once we have stood up to be counted, we have to leave people free to be what they want to be, even though we would prefer them to change. They are responsible for their conduct, we for ours. There is little point in going back over the past to see where we have failed because we might have done more. This makes guilt grow side by side with escalating fear which breeds remorse, achieving nothing but worry and anxiety for ourselves. When we speak the truth as we see it then we should be at inner peace, a peace within ourselves which nothing will disturb.

Discipline through example which flows from love is true discipleship. All through their lives parents will be honoured and respected by their children not because they are feared but because they are loved. Our healing services are geared to fostering a homely, loving, sharing Christian family in which God alone is the Father and Christ the head. Parents are really the elder brother and sister of the family. In our services, hundreds of families have been healed and freed from the 'control syndrome' where they are afraid to speak out or show their true feelings. Family life is all about personal relationships and the need to express love in its proper setting. One such person who was healed was Diane. She was never shown any love by her father. He seemed cold and devoid of emotion. After his wife's death he became even more withdrawn. I suggested to Diane that after the healing service she go home and tell him she loved him. This was to be her form of speaking out, with the risk of being rejected. It was a Saturday and when she got home she found him sitting comfortably in a chair watching football on the television. Diane hesitated at first then she went up to her father, put her arms round him and told him she needed his love. He cried and told her how lonely he was. That was the turning point in their lives. Diane and her father have been to many healing services since and they are so obviously happy that I know God has touched their lives. Parents need the love of children as much as children need theirs. While it is true that we need to be in control of our inner peace if we want to grow as persons, and that this is impossible without God's help, nevertheless, we also need the help of others, especially our family and friends. This means complete openness and sharing. Each of us is unique. A family should not only contain our differences, but foster them. The understanding of each other which is rooted in love will help us to grow in an awareness and acceptance of ourselves and each other.

My parents showed me by example what it was to be loved and not be afraid to show it. My father, long after I became a priest, was always at the railway station or the airport to give me a big hug. I can see him now with tears in his eyes as he held me close. He didn't care who saw us, I was his son and he my father. It was the same with my mother. She kissed us all each morning as we set off for school and she did the same on our return. I think I was about twelve when I asked her to stop doing this because I was getting 'too old' for it. Her reply was swift, 'You'll never be too old for that.' Thank God she never stopped showing her love for me. My parents taught me from my earliest years that freedom to be myself was one of the most important things in my life. It was easy to know and love God as my Father with parents such as mine. Through them I experienced the love of God which brings true freedom long before I ever read about it. God as my Father has always been real for me even in the times when I seemed to lose sight of him. I believe today because I caught my belief in my family and it has always been part of me. My sisters and brother trained me for the world in the unique struggle for survival and personal identity which is part and parcel of growing up in a loving family. In later life we still have memories of our moments of crisis when we laughed and cried together. These times will be forever special to us. They live on in me and I in them.

True freedom to be ourselves is fostered through love and not laws. It respects us as individuals and leads us as Christians into an awareness of God's love for us as a Father because of what we experience in our own family. The commandment of Christ to love one another as he has loved us is the essential witnessing sign of his followers: 'By this love you have for one another, everyone will know that you are my disciples.' (John 13:35) The

breakdown of love in the family and the apparent growing
delinquency of young people today is traceable to the
lack of essential sharing and caring necessary for those
who want to grow as persons, but have been deprived of
love in their family. The best way for parents to provide
for their children is to love them as God's special gifts to
them. This will be the children's greatest gift in later life.
They will learn from experience how to be fulfilled in
life and what it means to be in control of their inner
peace.

Love does not end in the family setting, but it should
begin there. We have to take the freedom to be and
to love ourselves that we have experienced in a human
Christian way out into our world, which to a large extent
has lost its way. It is in the noise and bustle of the market-
place that we witness to our Christian values. It is hard to
stand up and be counted among our friends and neighbours if we find that we seem to be a voice crying in the
wilderness. This is the time when fear tells us that we are
wasting our breath and it is best to remain silent. Standing
up for our set of values does not seem to do much good
anyway, so we are tempted to remain silent, to fade into
the crowd and become faceless people. Human approval
is the alluring siren that attracts us to the becalmed waters,
where we are beached, if not wrecked, on the rocks of
conformity. The quiet life on the surface hides the
dangerous currents underneath. I am always suspicious
when my inner life of peace is not threatened every so
often by people and situations round me. The Christian
life is a challenge to myself and my world and I cannot
settle for mediocrity. I know that it is only when I try to
live by my Christian faith that I am at peace and that
people take notice of who I am and what I stand for. I
dare to be different, not just for difference's sake, but
because I know in my conscience that I cannot conform
or surrender my freedom to anyone or any system. I
refuse to have my conscience controlled and silenced by

anyone. This control of people has become increasingly common in business in our depersonalised, materialistic society. People's security in earning their living is threatened and destabilised, making it more and more difficult for them to stand and be counted for what they believe to be right and necessary for their way of life. Edwin is a typical example of the many business people who come to us for our healing ministry. Here is his story:

'My life has been turned upside down these past ten years. It is all to do with my work and how things have changed so dramatically since then. Ten years ago I thought business prospects were bright, at least mine were. I was happily married with three wonderful children. I was, to say the least, comfortably placed, per-haps too comfortably. The future looked secure and there was nothing except the usual small things to worry about. I liked my work and there was a really good, friendly atmosphere among my colleagues. Then came the talk of a take-over. This changed everything; all of us took part in a survival operation because it was obvious that many of us would be expendable to the new company. The atmosphere changed in the office. Everyone became edgy and I was no exception. I worked from dawn to dusk, coming home exhausted and worried with no time or energy for my family. It was a stressful situation and I took it out on them. My marriage was threatened and our peaceful home was being torn apart by the work syndrome.

'I just did not know where to turn because I knew, deep down in my heart, that I was getting my priorities wrong. I looked round me in the office and I could see the obvious destructive effect it was having on all of us. I decided to talk things over, one evening, with my wife, Mary. We had a really good heart-to-heart sharing, and I came closer to her than I had done for years. She said that we should go to an inner healing service that was being held in a nearby parish church the following

Sunday. We went as a family. It was there that our lives began to change. The service was all about the true values in life and our need for inner peace. I knew then what we were missing. I was missing out on the quality of life. You came to me and told me to have the courage to change my pattern of life-style because that was the only way we would find happiness as a Christian family.

'When we got home, Mary and I decided on a course of action. I would work as normally as possible, giving myself time and space for the family and if this was not acceptable to my employers, than I would have to search for another job. When my boss called me in for an interview the following week and questioned me about my work, I told him what we had decided as a family. He was dumbfounded and was convinced that I had a much more lucrative post lined up for myself somewhere else! When I said 'no', he thought I was either lying or mad, but I assured him that I wanted to live a proper Christian family life and that this was impossible under the present excessively demanding working conditions. I could see in his eyes that he was kind of envious of what I wanted to do with my life.

'Out of the blue a few weeks afterwards, I was offered another job by a smaller firm. It was a mark down on my salary, but Mary, the children and I are infinitely happier. I can't begin to tell you of the change in our lives. People say I was lucky, but I believe that God was looking after me once I made my decision and took the plunge. It was our Christian faith which saved our marriage and our family. I may be poorer financially, but money cannot buy what we have found together.'

Edwin's story is a happy one, but I know hundreds of others like him whose lives are being wrecked on the business treadmill. They are being brought low by a system in which you either conform or are sidelined. Marriages are broken, families divided and the fabric of society is being shredded. I feel so sorry for the people trapped in such a situation and at El Shaddai we try to help them as best we can. When society loses sight of the individual and his right to grow as a person, then we are on the road to manipulation of people who are needed as fodder to keep the system going.

Yet we were born to live in a society where we could be ourselves. This is not possible where people are controlled. There has to be dialogue and it is here, I believe, that the Church must speak out boldly and clearly for those who have no one to speak for them. Churches are thriving spiritually in those parts of the world wherever and whenever they oppose injustice, and they are persecuted because they dare to speak out in the name of oppressed people. They are dying where they seem to ally themselves with manifestly corrupt regimes or remain silent in order to survive. When Christians speak out fearlessly in the cause of justice, then the rest of us take heart and the fire of Christian conscience within us is rekindled. The Church will witness effectively to the world only when it encourages true open dialogue within itself with all its own believers. It will not be afraid of the truth and will uphold the dignity of the human person and his conscience so that, together as fearless and committed Christians, we will proclaim the gospel to the world from the housetops. Whether or not it listens will not be due to our lack of conviction. What is important is that we will not be afraid in our situation, whatever it may be, to stand up and be counted!

10

Afraid to Make Friends

If we have never known love in our lives, then we are easy prey for all sorts of fear which will cripple and destroy us. We only come to really know ourselves through the love given to us. I was blessed with loving parents. What they taught me would not have made such a lasting impression on my life had I not been aware of their deep personal love for me. Through them I learned to love. They were the antidote to much of the false teaching about life and friendship. Their openness and friendship to others gave me the necessary assurance to reach out in love and friendship and to grow as a person. My life is warm in friendship, largely because of their influence. My friends have brought me so much light and laughter that whatever is good in me by God's grace has been nurtured by them. They have helped me to reach out to others without fear of what it will cost me in the process. I am less fearful today because of them.

> Anyone who claims to be in the light
>   but hates his brother
> is still in the dark.
> But anyone who loves his brother is living
>   in the light
> and need not be afraid of stumbling.
>   (1 John 2:9)

Fear breeds loneliness. It drains us of the joy of living

and destroys the sense of purpose and belonging which we all need in our lives. We were not meant to live in loneliness. Just as plants need water, we need friends. If we are to become alive and grow as persons then friends are a necessary part of our life and growth. This is a rule to which there is no exception. When no one loves and cares for us as a person, as we are in ourselves, then we feel unwanted and isolated, and insecure in ourselves. We are afraid of people and so find ourselves unable to take the risks of hurt involved in friendship.

Because Jesus was truly human he chose friends with whom he shared his life and mission. He said to his apostles, 'You are my friends . . . I shall not call you servants any more, because a servant does not know his master's business; I call you friends, because I have made known to you everything I have learnt from my Father. You did not choose me, no, I chose you' (John 15:15). Jesus needed friends in order to grow within himself. Some friends, like Peter, James and John, seem to have been more special to him than others. With them he shared his greatest joy on Mount Tabor and his deepest sorrow in the Garden of Gethsemane. Even though he spent much of his time alone in prayer, he was never lonely. He knew the danger of loneliness and the fear that it brings. In a special sense Jesus was the friend of everyone. He knew that in loving them he was doing exactly what his Father wanted him to do. His friendship for others had a healing quality which he passed on to and encouraged in his followers.

In our inner healing ministry we find that loneliness is the major cause of people's unhappiness and depression. Lonely people deep down may want to belong and share but they feel unable to do so. For various reasons, some of which are unknown to themselves, they are incapable of establishing true meaningful relations with other people. They just cannot make friends. They live on an island which is virtually impossible for outsiders to reach because of the dangerous currents of insecurity and perilous rocks of uncontrollable suspicion which surround it. As far as the world is concerned, lonely people are uncontactable offshore islanders. They may hunger for the nourishment of human company yet at the same time they reject it. They are emotionally and spiritually anorexic. Like anorexic people on a binge, they seem to be unable to retain the food of friendship which their personality so urgently needs. They live in a bubble which they are afraid will burst if they allow anyone else to share it with them. In their lives there is room for only one person, themselves. They may seem selfish but in reality they are enmeshed in chains which they cannot break.

The twentieth century is often called the century of the individual, the age of leisure and competition. It is also the age of loneliness. Of course we should love ourselves as individuals, but the world has so twisted the message that, in an age where there are more people than ever before sharing our universe, there are many who feel isolated and unhappy. Lonely people do not know – or even if they did, they don't want to live by the truth – that the only way to learn to love themselves is to love other people. If we are to become truly human and Christian then we have to journey outside ourselves in order to make contact with other people. Loving ourselves means loving other people. If we want to live in deep inner peace within ourselves, then we have to share ourselves with others. It is also true that it is essential for our inner peace of mind and heart that there are times when we need to be alone. If we share ourselves completely with others and never have time to be alone then we will have nothing left of ourselves, either for ourselves or for others. People today, however, tend to seek more and more privacy and yet they seem to feel more lonely and isolated when they get it. In reality they are not seeking privacy as much as isolation because they cannot face the challenges of making friends. Living in an insecure and self-seeking world they do not love themselves as they should. This makes them feel threatened by friendship because they are afraid that in the process of making friends they will lose something of themselves. Clinging to what they have, they are unable to reach out to others with the open hand of friendship. They live in a closed, secret garden whose gates are rusty because they have never been opened to admit friends.

Many people in today's world have an inner loveless emptiness. Human friendship at its deepest level is never allowed to enter this secret desolate place. Jesus is aware of our need of friendship because he knew his own human need to be loved. Three times he asked Peter, 'Simon son of John, do you love me?' (John 21:15–17). Jesus is the friend of the lonely, and he wants to lead them gently out of the prison which they have made for themselves. He knows the lonely have to be ready to share. He is patient as he says to them: 'Behold, I stand at the door and knock. If anyone hears my voice and opens the door, I will go in and sup with him, and he with me' (Revelation 3:20). In the depths of their being, lonely people hear the call, but they are afraid to answer because of the consequences involved. Once they love and are loved, they will no longer be alone and so they tend to feel they have lost something of themselves. Yet the only thing they will lose is their loneliness. They will have begun to share their life with other people. It is a whole new world of adventure and challenge.

Lonely people are sad inside, even though on the outside they may smile and look happy. They weep tears of the soul. They turn outwards to answer the cry that comes from deep within. They stop their ears and run away from the closed door, until the knocking becomes an ever-decreasing background sound, lost in the useless noise of a world which will not allow them to listen to themselves. They enact a modern 'Hound of Heaven' as they run away from themselves. They may have plenty of money and security and all the world has to offer, but in themselves they are empty. The bitter wind of loneliness blows through their lives, chilling them in their innermost being. They are afraid of getting old and being left alone. They become today's Midas, regretting that they ever asked for the power of the golden touch.

In our El Shaddai healing sessions I have been overwhelmed by the evidence of loneliness and lack of love in our materialistic world. People seem to have everything but love. Yet they need to be told that they are loved and wanted for themselves, and not for what they have or what they do. It is true love that really heals. Today we all need to reach our neighbour so that they will not feel alone, yet we are afraid to take the initiative. We too need to be touched, to feel the closeness of friendship of someone who is near, who is our friend. Knowing and acknowledging this need within ourselves should encourage us to reach out to lonely people so that they may come to know that what we offer them is genuine friendship for which we expect no return. We are someone with whom they can share and so free themselves from the fear of making friends and the power it holds over them. We need others as much as they need us.

Friendship changes our lives. It changed Elizabeth. This is how she described what happened when two people accepted her and offered her friendship: 'At the earliest age I can remember I knew instinctively that my parents did not want me. I was the classic unwanted baby. My mother left me for hours on my own, and my father never took the slightest notice of me. It was an unhappy home, with my parents constantly bickering. I never played with any children in the neighbourhood because already I was beginning to feel inadequate. At school everyone had friends except me. I was the odd one out and I spent play-time wandering around the school yard on my own. At home I was terrified of sleeping in the dark, and whenever I 'met' my parents I could not find words to express my deepest feelings of hurt. Things were much the same for years until I managed to get employment. I left home and rented a small flat, not so much to be free to do things, as much as to be on my own away from my parents. My flat became my prison. I loved it and hated it. What changed my life was a chance meeting with a middle-aged couple at church. In a way which I cannot explain, I started to talk to them about myself, gradually at first. They were so kind and understanding that I had not realised that there were people like that in the world. They invited me to their home for tea, and soon I became friends with their family. Friends for the first time! I could hardly believe it. My life changed, and it was all due to the gentleness and understanding of two people whom I had never met before but who could sense the emptiness and loneliness inside me. They changed my life. "Love changes everything." '

The human friendship offered to Elizabeth was the beginning of her healing as a person. Her new-found friends were Christian and as their friendship began to blossom they realised how deeply hurt Elizabeth was. They brought her to a healing service which for her was traumatic, even frightening. She needed to be healed of the hurtful memories of her childhood. Gradually she learned to forgive her parents, but this involved a long and painful process which included a shedding of many areas of bitterness in her life. In a sense she hated herself for not loving her parents, whereas she also needed to forgive them for not loving her. It was they who were the losers. Even today, five years after she first came to a healing service, there are times when she still feels the pain and rejection of years past. Instant healing of memories is extremely rare. What happened to us in our childhood will always remain part of us, which we need to control and grow through. Occasionally, hurtful memories will cast a cloud over our lives, but the sun of healing and forgiveness will soon break through to give us new warmth and hope. To forgive is always easier than to forget, and that is why lonely people need to be tended with great sensitivity and care. They are fragile. Their lives have made them so.

The healing of Elizabeth began with human friendship. Christian healing of a lonely person, while it is not a purely human process, nevertheless requires people to reach out to them as friends. Love, said Jesus, was to be the distinguishing mark of his followers. 'I give you a new commandment: love one another; . . . By this love you have for one another, everyone will know that you are my disciples.' (John 13:34–35) The healing Church of Christ will be the one which stresses the priority of caring, sharing friendship (love) among its followers. Christians yearn to see their Church as a loving extended family of which Christ is the loving head. They see him in those with whom they share their lives and mission. We all need a family or a community in which to live and grow as human beings. Our Christian faith is not just to bring people to God; it is also to bring people together. It is the Christian community trying to love as Christ did which ministers healing in his name. This is why we stress the *community* aspect of healing in all our El Shaddai services. We are a family who minister healing to each other in Christ's name because we are friends who care about each other and also bring people together. It binds us through love into a family in all aspects of our lives. God made us part of the human family. 'It is not good,' he said, 'for man to be alone' (Genesis 2:18). That is why he gave us each other so that through friendship for one another we might never feel isolated and alone. In and through each other we discover who we are and who God is. God wants us to see him as a loving Father. We do this by recognising him in the true Christian love we have for each other. Jesus was the visible sign of God's never-failing healing love for everyone. He told Philip, 'to have seen me is to have seen the Father' (John 14:9).

At a purely human level people are afraid to show

loving friendship for each other. Christian institutions which stress the importance of 'loving God above all things' often miss out on the necessity of loving people as well. Father Jim's love of God was like that. I met him some thirty years ago when I gave a retreat to missionaries in Africa. He was an exact man, scrupulous in attending to every detail of his priestly duties as a missionary. Another priest told me, 'You could set the clock by him.' There was nothing on the outside to suggest the turmoil inside this shell of a man. He admitted to me that he never really loved anyone because he was afraid of being rejected. He said that life for him was sheer misery since he kept everyone at arm's length from his affection and confidence. He had, as it were, a large sign placed in front of him: 'Trespassers will be prosecuted.' He had become a professional dispenser of sacraments – a human slot-machine. He was loveless and lifeless. He took consolation in performing his tasks with great care and attention to detail so that everything went according to the book. He never saw people as individuals to love, but only in terms of how they stood with regard to the discipline of the Church. His parishioners respected him, but few loved him because he would not allow them to get to know him. He did not really love himself and saw God as a judge who would scrutinise every iota of his life. He was afraid of losing his vocation as a priest if he drew too close to others. Yet he was destroying his priestly ministry by his refusal to let go and trust the Lord. We laid hands on him in the healing ministry and prayed for him. He started to weep, gently at first, and then the tears came in a great flood. It took many sessions for Father Jim to be helped and healed. He told me that any demonstration of affection was taboo in his house. From school he went straight to a seminary. During the holidays he either kept to himself or mixed only with other young clerical students aspiring to the priesthood. All he ever knew was the Church's clerical life, and outside it he was lost. The process of his healing was most exhausting and sensitive. The gentleness of God as he set Father Jim free to stretch his eagle's wings is something which will stay with me all my life. There are many like Father Jim and Elizabeth who need our love and friendship if they are to overcome the fear which cripples their lives.

Fear tells us, as it so obviously told Father Jim, that love or deep friendship is not for us. We cannot trust ourselves because of the destructive hidden forces within us, and we certainly cannot trust others because they are fostering the friendship only for what they can get out of it for themselves. It takes longer to build barriers than to knock them down, and so in our fear for ourselves and our distrust of others we man the barriers to keep deep friendship out of our lives. The number of people who live by this horrendously distrustful code is alarmingly high, and it is a perfect feeding ground for fear. Is it any wonder that highly institutionalised communities look with suspicion on the healing ministry and hear alarm bells ring at the words 'freedom to be yourself'. Those who foster this negative teaching on friendship must bear the responsibility for the many people crippled by hang-ups on sex and irrational guilt. If sex is the never-ending relentless theme of our teaching and the most dangerous pitfall for us as Christians, then the foundation is well and truly laid for a narrow introverted outlook on life, the Church, the world and God. We will be frenetically aware of a just God never taking his eyes off us as we walk the tightrope of our earthly existence. We will be acutely afraid of toppling over unless we are constantly on our guard to keep ourselves perfectly balanced. If that is how we see life, then is it any wonder that so many jump off because they feel that too much is being asked of them. When love not sex, trust not fear, is predominant in our teaching, the joy of the gospel will spill over into the lives of our congregations. We will know a love for God and each other which casts out fear. We will trust each other because we know that we are trusted. We will be free to make friends and put aside our loneliness.

Lack of trust is one of the most destructive elements in the life of the institutional Church. If the institution does not trust me, than I am being taught not to trust those within it. In this way we Christians distrust each other and the devil makes mayhem of all our ideals. The institution that does not live and preach trust condemns itself in the light of Christ's gospel. *Ubi caritas et amor deus ibi est* – 'Where love and trust abide, there is God.' The early Christians were known by their love rather than by their efficiency and bureaucratic government. The institutional Church, when it trusts me, heals me in a way that its rules never could. Stringent, minute and restrictive rules are too hygienic and sterile for human growth. The loving doctor cures his patient so that they can lead as full a life as possible in the world *outside* the hospital. The Church which is positive and trusting, heals and helps me for my life in the world. This may be a wicked world but our lives should redeem it. St Paul prayed for the Philippians that they might be 'innocent and genuine, perfect children of God among a deceitful and underhand brood, and you will shine in the world like bright stars . . .' (Philippians 2:14).

Freedom is a word which chills fearful people because it takes away from them the security of their own private, personal prison. Yet friendship based on trust is necessary for all forms of healing. When we offer genuine love or friendship to others, then we are setting them free to live their lives as whole persons. In this way we are preparing them for healing. Healing leads to wholeness, and the measure of our lives as Christians is the number of people whom we have helped to find, with God's grace, their wholeness as persons. I can never understand why we are told that we are not to get involved with people, as if God distrusts all forms of human friendship. Without meaning to, we are subconsciously saying that all friendship has illicit sexual overtones. Freud has become our mentor, not Jesus who publicly mixed with the sinners and drop-outs of his world. Thomas à Kempis, the well-known con-templative monk, wrote in 'The Imitation of Christ' that the more he went out among men the less he came back a man. Whom did he meet and what happened to make him have such a negative attitude to people and the world in which he lived? If my fear of the world is dominated by a distrust of all forms of emotional involvement, then I shall never really trust anyone's show of emotion, least of all my own. I wonder why Jesus wept so openly over the death of his friend Lazarus, considering he would within an hour restore him to life again. By being fully human, fully alive, Jesus the healer shows us that, like the couple who befriended Elizabeth, our loving contact with others gives them the power to love themselves by nourishing in them a true sense of their own worth in their own eyes. For them life really becomes worth living since love transforms life. All true friendship has a healing effect, both on the person who offers and the one who receives it. When I offer my friendship to someone I am saying, in fact: 'I am your friend with no strings attached. It does not matter what you do or have done. I want to be always there with and for you, whether you need me or not. Don't ask me why. Just be happy, as I am, that I value your friendship as something very important in my life. I commit myself to you so that my life is fuller because of our friendship. I want to become "your friend" rather than for you to be "my friend". This means that I want what is best for you. I want to set you free to be yourself, to become fully alive. I am sensitive to your value as a unique part of the mystery and glory of God's world. I do not desire to become your whole life for your horizons may differ from mine. My wish is for you to experience all the joys of your world, and in your happiness I too find happiness. You owe me nothing, and if you can say "I am glad I am me", then your difference from me in many things does not in any way threaten our friendship. We have helped each other to come alive and for this I praise the Lord. He alone is your world and mine.'

True caring for the other person in genuine friendship means that I want him to be more whole, more his true self. My friendship unlocks the door of his prison and sets him free to venture out into the world with confidence and hope that he will find others to love and be loved by. God has given us all within our deepest being the desire and capacity to love. We need someone other than ourselves to activate this innate power. It is for this reason that God our Father sent his son Jesus into our world so that through his love for others the love of the Christian family might be set in motion. His love touched other people and made them come alive. We too are to share in Christ's healing love so that our contact with others will enable them to be free to enjoy life in the company of friends. We may never see them again or have the same close union with them, but we are pleased that God has used us to open for them a whole new world of Christian friendship. We may not be conscious of what we are doing, and perhaps it is better that way. We are just being ourselves, sharing with others the joy of Christian friendship which we in our turn received from others. In our healing ministry I constantly stress that we must never offer friendship which has selfish overtones. This is a 'friendship' which is manipulative and destructive of people who come to us for the ministry of healing. In the guise of offering friendship we take from them the little love and trust they have to offer and leave them even more wounded in their personality. Instead of wanting them to be gradually the kind of person God wants them to be, we expect, even demand, that they immediately live the life we plan for them. Let me share a story with you which explains what I mean.

John, a Protestant, and Helen, a Catholic, from Belfast found life intolerable after their marriage. Neither their family nor their community would accept them. After years of hassle, in a moment of desperation they fled the country with their two children, one a young baby only three months old. They ended up on my doorstep without money or even a change of clothing for their baby. They were a refugee family and in them I saw clearly the modern example of Mary and Joseph with the infant Jesus. A supportive group of Christians of all denominations, which I had formed for such emergencies, gave them all the necessary help we could muster. It was wonderful to see how unselfish these Christians were in giving of themselves to this frightened family. Nothing was too much for our group. A house was found, then furniture and clothing, and finally employment for the father. It was a joy to see the transformation that took place in this young family because of unselfish, human Christian caring. Within a few weeks a Pentecostal group visited the family and welcomed them along to their church. They appeared to be friendly, but when the family did not turn up for service the following Sunday they were promptly dropped. The angry parents asked me, 'Why did they come? Were they just interested in recruiting more members for their church?' Their visitors were proselytisers, not Christians. They were interested in systems, not people. As Christians we are interested in people for their own sake. It is our privilege and duty to help, whatever the outcome.

If only we could see into the future we would be amazed at the hidden influences for good that Christian friendship has on people's lives. Frightened people give little just because they are afraid. When we really love them they will come out of their burrows like rabbits, timid at first, but gradually they will play in the open fields in the sunlight, knowing they have nothing to fear. Our world is startlingly full of frightened people who do not want to be hurt any more. People hurt each other, so what reason have they for trusting us? They are damaged people who

feel they are in a sense society's lepers. They still need
caring for like those who cried out to Jesus, 'Sir . . . if you
want to, you can cure me.' . . . Jesus said, 'Of course I want
to! Be cured!' (Luke 5:13) One of the most precious gifts
we can give to one another in friendship is our capacity
to listen in love to someone who has difficulty in explain-
ing what is hurting them deep inside. It is one quality for
whose lack of use we can all strike our breasts. We excuse
ourselves by saying we are 'too tired', 'no, not again', or
'my goodness, don't people realise I have a life of my
own'. Yet when I make myself available to listen to
another, I am saying: 'I am listening to you now. Forget
how long it takes. You just tell me about yourself in your
own way and at your own pace. I don't want to be anywhere else but here with you. You are my world and its
centre is you. Let me be the mirror in which you can see
yourself perhaps more clearly than before. My mind and
heart are with you because I want desperately to feel what
you feel. I want to make contact with you so that you can
make contact with yourself.' In this process of dialogue,
during which I may say nothing, I come across a new
discovery of myself in another, in which the damaged
person becomes my mirror in which I see my own imper-
fections. It is a case of 'physician heal thyself'. The discoveries in medicine depend on the illnesses of patients.
It is the same with Christian healing. We are healed by
those who come to us for healing. There is no one
involved in the ministry of healing who is not constantly
in need of healing himself.

An illustration of 'listening in depth' is the case of a
young father who had just been told that he was critically
ill with cancer, and I was asked to visit him. We had met
only once before. As I entered the ward I found him lying
on his bed looking at the ceiling in fear and disbelief at
what had overtaken him: I sat there and just waited until
he was ready to tell me about his worries. No drugs
seemed to bring him rest, so I took his hand in mine and

projected myself into his situation. Soon I saw myself in him and in some inexplicable way I was experiencing to some degree his emotions. Together we came through his crisis point. He was no longer withdrawn. Together we had both experienced a beautiful and unique situation. He had a peace within him which I knew I did not give. He lost his fear of being open about his illness and from then onwards he saw everything in a new and wonderful way. He lived with his cancer, a quality of life which only God could bestow on him as a special gift.

People are often afraid to make friends because they have been hurt by those whose offer of friendship was superficial. This happened to John and Helen. The church people who came to visit them *talked at them* instead of *listening, then talking to them*. Where there is no listening there is no dialogue. When Jesus said 'blessed are your ears' (Matthew 13:16) he meant also that we are blessed if we listen with our hearts as well as our heads. In that way we talk heart to heart, deep to deep. We just have *to be* to those who are lonely and frightened. They see behind the words, or silence, to our friendship which like a gentle sun will melt away the coldness they feel inside. The more of ourselves we are prepared to reveal the more we encourage others to be themselves in honest, open dialogue. In our encounter we too experience inner healing. If we hold back anything of ourselves which we are not prepared to reveal then we are to that extent not listening. However, the healing of frightened, lonely people is a slow, sensitive process. Love will get through eventually when everything else fails. There are so many people, ourselves included, who need to be 'loved better'. Every encounter in true friendship heals us. In our friends we find the loving Christ, friend of everyone.

11

Afraid to Trust God in the Bad Times

Uncontrolled fear destroys trust. When we are in its grip, we find it almost impossible to trust anyone. We have been let down so many times in the past by so-called friends that when a crisis enters our life we shrink in on ourselves. Our instinct tells us that it is better to keep our own counsel rather than risk being hurt again. If this is true of our human relationships, then what about trusting God when we are overburdened by something which so overpowers and preoccupies us that the very idea of asking God to help us never enters our mind? Fear tells us that he too has let us down in the past, even when we have stormed heaven with prayers which he never seems to answer. So why trust him now? We panic in a crisis, our peace is disturbed, and so trusting God to help us is outside the frontiers of our situation. Fear, not faith, is in control.

We often say very glibly that we trust God with our lives, but this is easier said than done. It is easy to trust him when things are going well for us but what about our trust when everything in our lives seems to be falling apart? What about trust then, when it is winter, not spring, and we wander in a desert and not a scented garden? This is the time when we have to live by faith because this is all that is left to us. I know because I have been there.

It is a time for reading and living the gospel with new vision and seeing how Jesus coped during his life, doing whatever God wanted him to do, especially when he was faced with hatred, suspicion, jealousy and violence on all sides. How did he cope then with his fears? He is our example and hope on those occasions in life when we feel lost and wonder who will help us and who cares about our situation. The apostles were in a situation like that when a sudden storm on a lake seemed to threaten their lives. The boat was nearly swamped, but Jesus was sleeping peacefully in the boat's stern. They woke him and said to him 'Master, do you not care? We are going down!' Of course Jesus cared, after all they were his specially chosen friends. When he had 'calmed the sea' he said to them, 'Why are you so frightened? Have you still no faith?' (Mark 4:39–40)

Jesus, the man of faith, lived out his life in complete trust. No matter what happened to him in the bad times as well as the good, he never lost his inner peace. Why? Because he looked on God as his Father to whom he had committed his whole life. 'The Father and I are one,' he said (John 10:30). He was speaking as a man because 'he did not cling to his equality with God' (Philippians 2:6). As a man he lived in the shadow of a cross so that we would see him as a pilgrim walking in the valley of darkness. If we say it was all right for him because he was God then we are denying that he was truly a man who in suffering had his faith and trust in God put to the test. He put his oneness with his Father before any personal calamity. Through his trust in God in all his trials he was bearing witness to his Father's never-failing love. This was the cornerstone of his trust and faith. God as his Father, and he as God's son in human flesh, were the perfect team who would always overcome whatever the odds.

Jesus lived out his life from beginning to end doing whatever the Father wanted him to do. Even at the tender age of twelve he was so completely in tune with his Father's will for him that he stayed behind in the Temple of Jerusalem, without his mother knowing it, 'sitting among the doctors, listening to them and asking them questions' (Luke 2:46). When his mother scolded him for causing her such unnecessary worry, he made no excuse or apologies. He replied quite simply, 'Why were you looking for me? Did you not know that I must be busy with my Father's affairs?' But they did not understand what he meant.' (Luke 2:49–50) Jesus had one objective in mind from which he never deviated even though he was often misunderstood. 'My food,' he said, 'is to do the will of the one who sent me, and to complete his work.' (John 4:34)

Jesus *knew* God not only *by faith* but also *by experience*. He was his Father at work in all that he said and did. From the age of twelve he was also aware that there were many Pharisees and rabbis who studied religion and *knew* a lot *about* God but *did not know him, experience him* as a person. They were well-versed in religion; that was their business. They were, however, lightweight in matters of faith. Religion teaches us about God. It is a way of rule rather than life. Faith is God's gift alone by which we become aware of him as someone supremely important in our lives. For Jesus he was a loving Father whom once you know, and experience, your life is changed. You will then know what it is to seek his kingdom first. Deep in your heart you will want to make him known for who he is and what he means to us. This is what inspired Jesus to say to his apostles in his farewell discourse: 'Father, Righteous One, the world has not known you, but I have known you, and these have known that you have sent me. I have made your name known to them and will continue to make it known, so that the love with which you loved me may be in them, and so that I may be in them.' (John 17:25–26)

The Hebrew word for 'knowing' in the text is *yadha*

which really means loving, being one with the other person. Jesus was perfectly in love with his Father and was in a unique position to tell us about him so that we too might know and love him as our Father also. When we suffer and still go on believing, trusting, in the loving fatherhood of God, then we are in the process of growing as Christians. What we have learned about God is tested in the crucible of a crisis of suffering so that what remains is faith, even though for a short time we must bear all sorts of trials so that the worth of our faith, more valuable than gold may be proved. (1 Peter: 6–7).

Let me tell you a story of when religion gave way to faith and trust in God. It concerns Elizabeth. This is what she wrote to me: 'For as long as I can remember, I was a respected and respectable member of church and state. My parents were pillars of the church and so was I. Church-going was very much an integral part of our family life. I married John from my local church and everything in the garden was rosy. We were not what you would call wealthy, but we were definitely not short of this world's goods. I was a local magistrate and thought I had nicely balanced my life between my home and my outside commitments. We have two children who are the joy of our lives. It seemed too good to be true. I was convinced that I believed in God and never forgot to thank him for his goodness to us. I was a Christian, or so I thought.

'The bubble burst. Two years ago I lost my father through cancer just at a time when I felt he could really enjoy his retirement, when I would be able to do more for him. I never remember him being ill. He went to his doctor for his normal medical check-up and in less than three months he was gone from us. I found it hard to see my mother grieve so much. Then my daughter got ME in her first year at university, and to crown it all my husband, John, was made redundant. We were all shattered. My ivory tower was in ruins.

'I went to church as usual but found little peace there.

The services were meaningless. I was not angry with God. He was irrelevant to me. I wonder if I ever believed in him. One day in desperation I went to our church and sat at the back, looking up at the altar. My eyes were drawn to the figure on the cross. I had seen it for many years, but had never really noticed it before. I started talking to him, saying, 'Do you know how I feel? How I am? I feel lost. Why don't you help me?' Then it seemed as if the crucified Christ was looking at me and saying, 'In my wounds you are healed. The darkness will pass. You will walk in the light again.' I fell on my knees and the tears began to fall. I don't know how long I stayed there. All I do know is that afternoon I found my Christ and my God. I still have my problems but now my life has taken on a new meaning. Now I know what it is to believe and trust in God.'

There is a crisis moment for all of us when we are challenged by events in our life. They do not announce their coming, which makes their presence among us all the more difficult to bear and to understand. We may even ask ourselves why God allows such nasty things to happen to good people. We are stopped in our tracks. We have to make a choice because we are in a crisis. Crisis means growing-point. This is the time when we grow out of religion into faith, when God becomes a real person, our loving Father, and Christ becomes our Lord and friend. In the El Shaddai ministry we encourage people to grow and, through the gospel experience in their lives, to really know God and not just a lot of rules and words about him.

Fear, however, which is opposed to the trust born of faith, does not want us to grow as persons. It prevents us from facing up to the challenge to move forward with our lives. It drags us back into the past where it reminds us of previous failures and the times when we trusted God with the outcome, only to find that he let us down. We keep what we have left of our independence and battle through as best we can on our own resources, trusting nobody.

Gregory is a typical example of this negative attitude. He was an alcoholic whose drinking habits destroyed his personal life. His wife and family stayed with him as long as they could until finally, for their own safety, even sanity, they had to leave him. Gregory felt very sorry for himself and blamed them for turning their backs on him when he needed them most. Blaming others for your own shortcomings and mistakes is a typical symptom of someone who is lacking in responsibility and trust and picks someone as a scapegoat. Soon Gregory lost any friends he had except those who shared his weakness for drink. He came to an El Shaddai healing service and seemed to be very moved by the experience. He promised that he would never touch another drop of drink again, but I warned him that his optimism and confidence in himself were misplaced. He did not evaluate the situation properly. I did not see him again for some time, but during this period he wrote effusive letters of how God had helped him to conquer the 'demon drink'. It seemed to be a miracle, but unfortunately it was not so. He rang me late one evening, much the worse for wear and began to attack God, me and other Christians for letting him down. He was 'back on the bottle' worse than ever before. He had claimed a 'healing' all too quickly. Apparently he went with friends to a birthday party at which he thought he might be 'safe' with a little whisky, which proved to be his undoing. Gregory trusted himself too much and in a crisis went back to his old habits. Trust in God means that we know and accept our own limitations, and with his help we can move forward in our lives to a new purpose. It also makes us aware that in our crisis we know him and acknowledge our need of his help and love. Gregory thought he knew God but he forgot to learn to know himself.

Once we really know God as a loving Father our lives

take on a new dimension. We are no longer alone. We *know* we have a Father who loves us and wants what is best for us. We are *one* with God the Father through Christ's love for us both. We trust, have confidence in, each other. When suffering comes our way, through this trust in him we are able to talk to him about what disturbs us much as a child does with a loving parent. In our suffering, of course, we should ask the question, 'Why me, Lord?' We should ask God our Father for an understanding in faith of what is happening to us and why. After all, we trust him with our lives. We are in the battlefield of suffering where often, in the mist of conflict, friend and foe are confused. We tussle with God until he quietens us, and when we are still he holds us in his arms and brings us his Son's gift of peace.

All suffering must be examined in the light of the gospel. Suffering may so limit us as persons that it brings life at every level to a standstill. It may destroy our faith in God as a Father who seems to abandon us when we are wounded like birds with broken wings. At times we need to remind ourselves that Jesus came on earth to heal and to ensure that we would live life as fully as possible. He healed because this is what his Father wanted him to do. Then why do we suffer? Couldn't God abolish suffering altogether? If he loves us and has the power to do it, why is there so much pain in our world and our lives? The answer is not simple and involves total faith and trust.

There is an apparent contradiction, a paradox, between suffering and healing which is perfectly illustrated in Christ's own life. He did not want to suffer and die on a cross. He prayed, 'Father, if you are willing, take this cup away from me. Nevertheless, let your will be done, not mine.' (Luke 22:42) He endured the cross in faith and trust, believing that in his suffering God the Father would heal the world in a way which he did not fully understand. There is a hidden Christian value in suffering which is a mystery even to Christ, who knew his Father better than anyone else. He hung on the cross in faith and trust.

For Jesus the important thing in his life was to trust his Father. He never looked on suffering as sent by a God who gloried in pain. If suffering came, then for Jesus it had to have a positive, creative, spiritual meaning. After his resurrection he reminded his apostles, 'So you see how it is written that the Christ would suffer and on the third day rise from the dead, and that, in his name, repentance for the forgiveness of sins would be preached to all the nations' (Luke 24: 46–47). The only suffering of any value for Christ is the suffering willingly and lovingly endured in faith and trust, otherwise suffering for him is destructive of our emotional, physical and spiritual lives. Christ saw healing in suffering. It is only when we begin to understand healing that our perception of the mystery of suffering will grow. In trust we have to discern that suffering will help us to grow as a person because of our attitude to it. We should never accept suffering blindly; we have to soak it in the healing ointment of faith and trust.

Health and healing is what God wants for his people, and we have an *obligation* as Christians to pray for it. Healing was one of the most important ministries of a young Church eager to evangelise and spread the healing gospel of Jesus Christ. If we have neglected it then we have failed countless millions of people who, because of our lack of faith, have been deprived of God's healing power and love. Christ never withdrew his promise to his followers, 'I tell you most solemnly, whoever believes in me will perform the same works as I do myself, he will perform even greater works' (John 14:12). Personally, I have no hesitation in praying for healing for someone suffering from a physical or emotional disorder once I discern that, as far as my faith and understanding go, this is what God wants for them. In trust I leave the end result to him. I know that God will always heal even though it may not be in the way the person or I want. God alone knows what his child needs, and no prayer is ever left unanswered. Let me tell you a story to illustrate this:

Charles came to a healing service with his wife. His body was shot through with cancer and he was given only a few months to live. He was obviously shattered by the medical diagnosis, and just could not accept it. He and his wife wanted an instant cure. I knew that he was filled with fear and worry, and so I prayed for his inner peace, assuring him that God loved him. He went away hoping that he was cured. In a month's time he was back again at our healing service. I asked him to let the peace of the service soak into his soul. After Mass when I prayed with him he was much more open to experiencing God the Father's love for him. Afterwards he wrote to me, saying, 'I am living with cancer, not dying from it. My life, and that of my wife, is changed. We know God loves us. Nothing will ever take that away from us. We have really come alive these past five weeks and our relationship together is just wonderful. If I had never known cancer, I would never have experienced such love and peace.' Of course Charles and his wife pray for a physical cure, and why not? No matter what happens they know that through the mystery of suffering and healing they have entered the garden of peace where the risen Jesus walks in the morning air. This is the basis of their hope and trust. They are healed as persons.

Jesus was Father-oriented. His Father was the centre of his life. His knowledge and love of his Father fed each other. If we took all his references to the Father in his discourses and stories out of the gospel there would be little left. In fact there would be no gospel of substance, no good news. In the Christian faith we highlight the great unselfish love that Jesus had for his followers, and yet this is only a reflection of the love which the Father had for Jesus: 'As the Father has loved me, so I have loved you.' (John 15:9) Our love for Christ is the gateway to the love of God the Father which is beyond our wildest dreams and imagining. 'Anyone who loves me will be loved by my Father.' (John 14:21)

Christ is our example of how to love and trust God as a Father. God, however, is not *personally* loved by many church-going people as the Father should be loved. We keep his commandments and do what we have to do, perhaps even a bit more, but there is no joy of exciting love in our relationship with him. We expect him to reward the good and punish the wicked, much as the elder brother expected in the story of the prodigal son (Luke 15:25–32). We forget that God wants to be loved. This is the only meaningful service that he wishes from us. Service without love is a discipline of drudgery and not a discipleship of love. It drains life of freedom and joy.

We will never grow as Christians, and our service of God will never have the authentic ring of freedom, until we allow God to be our Father so that our love for him is as personal as that of Jesus. For Jesus he was a personal Father. He must be the same for us. The greatest healing needed today in all Christian churches is to be open to God the Father's unique love for all his people. The main function of the Christian churches is to encourage their people to be aware of God's fatherly love for them. We do not love the Church for itself but only in so far as it helps us to love God. A church which is not transparently God-conscious and Father-loving is a bureaucratic shell without life or purpose.

God's love for us never ebbs or flows. When we sin it is not God but we ourselves who have erected the barrier between us. For us in El Shaddai our main platform on which all healing is built is the wounded person's awareness of God's love for us as a Father. Without it we can make no progress. This is why I am opposed to those who rush into healing someone as if it were a fast-food meal instead of something very delicate and fragile. No one is able to minister healing at a deep level unless and until they are aware of God as their Father and that it is he alone who heals. It is especially important to become aware of God the Father's love for us all where the person coming for help has never been aware of a parent's love in their family life. Mary is a typical example. She has been to our healing services many times and I have watched her life blossom and grow.

'There was no love in our home. I never had any affection shown to me by either of my parents. My father was a good man but I often felt he should never have married. He would have been better off as a bachelor. My mother never seemed to be able to cope with life and was afraid of everyone and everything. My brother and sister were scrubbed clean for church on Sunday. It was the done thing, the external sign that we were a good, God-fearing family. The church services, like the congregation, were cold and rather forbidding. When my sister became pregnant she had to leave home 'because of the neighbours'. I think she grabbed at the first bit of affection which was shown her.

'A few years afterwards I felt I was on the verge of a nervous breakdown. Even though I was not a Catholic, I heard from a friend of mine that there was a healing service at her church. I was so desperate, I was prepared to try anything once, even going to a Catholic church. What a change it made in my life. The service was all about God the Father's love for us. Everyone seemed so happy, friendly and relaxed. They were enjoying themselves, which I thought you never did in church. Then you prayed over me, and laid your hands gently on my head. No one ever touched me like that before. It was a new experience.

'I went home and found my mother busy as usual doing something about the house, anything to keep her occupied. I gave her a cup of tea and asked if I could talk with her. She didn't know what to do. Anyway, to cut a long story short, our house is now a loving home. I get on much better with my mother and father. It took them a long time to get used to the change in me. I thought there is no point in loving God as my Father if I don't show love to my parents. My sister and her lovely son are now made really welcome. Who and what changed us? God the Father's love.'

Mary worried endlessly about her poor relationship with her parents. In the end, as a result of the healing service, she trusted God. She knew she had to take the initiative once she felt that she had sufficient inner peace and strength to do so. She knew that worrying about her problem did not solve it and so she asked God to help her and guide her as to what she should do to remedy the situation. Mary knew that trust and worry are poor bedfellows. Worry is destructive of trust. It breeds anxiety and tension. Jesus reminds us that if we really trust God as our Father then we have no cause for worry. Of course we have problems and we have to face up to them responsibly, but we should never allow them to take control and get out of hand. Worry divides us. It gives us too heavy a burden to carry, one which weighs down our inner peace. God the Father knows our needs when we are too preoccupied with our wants. Jesus gives us a recipe for inner peace.

The only path to inner peace is to believe that our Father loves us more than we love ourselves. We have to learn to surrender all our problems, big and small, to God. When we talk with him in prayer he will provide the answer. He is my Father who wants me secure and happy in his love. From my own experience I know that in the final analysis God has never failed me in the past and I have no reason for thinking that he will fail me in the future. The future is in God's hand. It is his world, his people, his Church. They couldn't be in better, more loving hands. But I also know that I shall always need his loving guidance because I cannot go it alone. Left to myself I would soon fall flat on my face. I am aware that past failures have been my fault, even though at the time I was angry with God and blamed him for the things that went wrong in my life.

We all have problems. God preserve us from the person who has not. Troubles come our way; we do not have to invite them into our lives. A death in the family, a lack of faithfulness in one we love, a separation in marriage, the loss of employment, a physical or mental sickness which changes our accustomed life pattern, and a thousand and one sad events take us into the desert of loneliness so that we are thrown off balance. We are tempted to worry because we cannot visualise how we can cope with our problems, or see the road ahead. For a while we lose our grip on inner peace. These are the storms in life which test whether or not the house of self is built on the rock of faith and trust in God or on the sand of selfishness. When an unexpected problem disrupts the smooth flow of our lives, our Christian faith is being examined. We are being tested. The quality of our peace will soon be seen for what it is. How often have I seen people who go to church week after week unable to cope with a situation which requires deep faith and trust in God. They took God for granted and never thought that they would run into problems which they could not solve without him. Faith, not religion, dilutes and dissolves the oil slick of worry which clogs up our life.

When I trust God with all of my life, the bad as well as the good, then fear will never control me. If I worry or am anxious about how I can cope with my problems, then I am relying on my own resources and not on God's. As a Christian I am never alone. God who put me in this situation can change it. In other words, today's situation with its problems will not be the same tomorrow, and when tomorrow comes it ceases to be tomorrow; it becomes today, in which God is with me every moment. Tomorrow I shall just have to look at how the situation will be then, because it is the problem I shall have to cope with in the here and now. I trust the future to God, my Father in love, just as I commit my past to his mercy. It is really the only way to live and keep inner peace.

12

Afraid of the Past and Hurtful Memories

Guilt and fear are a dangerous cocktail. They leave us with such a destructively painful hangover that we are unable to live our lives in peace and happiness. It is as if we were perpetually living out the morning after the night before, spent in the darkness of guilt which overpowers us, and which, like an alcoholic, we find it impossible not to indulge in. The darkness is a result of things that happened in our lives in the past of which we are ashamed. They are the skeletons in our cupboard which, however much we pretend are not there, nevertheless every so often rattle and make us aware of their frightening presence. They mock us and fill us with such irrational guilt that we are unable to be at peace within ourselves. Of all the healing we need most if we are to grow as persons, then surely we have to learn to forgive ourselves. If we don't, then we cannot live in the present moment because false guilt holds us to ransom. We are its prisoner whom it refuses to let free. Even though we may wander apparently freely in the world throughout the day, guilt reminds us that when the shadows lengthen we are nothing but escaped convicts who have been given life sentences because of our past actions. Guilt and fear are the unbreakable chains which bind us to the past. This description of guilt may sound dramatic, but I have encountered hundreds of people whose lives are tortured by irrational guilt. They are the prisoners whom Jesus came to set free (Luke 4:18).

John was such a prisoner for as long as he could remember. When I first met him he was a broken man, even though, to all outward appearances, he seemed perfectly normal and happy. I knew when I looked in his eyes that he was tortured inside. He was saying in his heart, 'Please help me. In the name of God set me free from the past. Let me know happiness.' I could hear his unspoken cry for help and so I prayed with him and asked him to be gentle with himself because whatever was wrong in his life was already forgiven. 'It's my past, Father,' he whispered in my ear. 'I can't get away from it. It haunts me. I just can't forgive myself.' His memories of the past would not allow him to live at peace with himself in the present. I helped him quietly to go back into the past, but not alone. He was to allow Jesus to accompany him as his friend. Together, over many sessions, we conquered his guilt over the sexual misbehaviour of his youth. He realised, probably for the first time in his life, that forgiveness of himself was the only way in which he could overcome the guilt which was destroying his life. If we don't forgive ourselves, then we cannot forgive anyone else. If we want to be healed of the hurt we have caused others, or the hurt which they have inflicted on us, then it is forgiveness which is the key to our peace and wholeness. John's faith came alive when he believed that God was his Father who really loved, understood and forgave him. He saw the crucifixion of Christ not so much as a condemnation of what his personal sin had done to God's Son, but rather as a sign of Christ's love, not only for his Father, but also for him. John knew at last that it was true that by Christ's wounds he was healed.

He was only too well aware of how destructive of his peace it was to wallow in the past as if Christ had not come to do away with sin. John gradually learned to apply the wounds of Christ to his own situation and in them he found the ointment for his healing. He knew what his *real* guilt was because of his sins, but he had got it out of proportion. As we magnify guilt we minimise forgiveness. We forget that God 'takes our sins farther away than the East is from the West' (Psalm 103:12) and nothing could be farther than that. Irrational guilt, on the other hand, locks the sin into our memory so that it poisons our life. It destroys us at every level – spiritual, emotional and physical. If Christian peace demands that we forgive our enemy, then we are also obliged to forgive ourselves and to stop destroying ourselves by false guilt which is the enemy within. If we do not forgive ourselves then we will not experience inner peace. Memories of the past which fill us with false guilt are the alien force within gnawing away at our peace continually so that our thoughts increasingly revolve round them. Until we forgive ourselves for sins of the past, then we will not be able to live the Christian life which looks on God as a loving Father.

Just as we forgive the wrongs others have done to us, then why forget to forgive ourselves? John became so wrapped up in his guilt that he had a very poor appreciation of himself as a person. Guilt from the past was preventing him from having a proper respect for himself as the person he was at the present period of his life. He found it extremely difficult to forget because feeling guilty had become an integral part of his life. Whenever the guilt processes started up again, I got him to repeat the words of Jesus, 'leave the dead to bury their dead' (Matthew 8:22). He had to believe that he was forgiven, which is why whenever he uncovered his sin, he had to reaffirm his belief that his guilt was destroyed by the cross of Christ which, like a stake, had driven itself into the vampire of false guilt and had destroyed it. The vampire of false guilt cannot live in the light of Christ's love for us.

John was right to feel guilty about the sins which he

had committed, but needed to believe that they were forgiven. There are many others, however, who also feel the same remorseless sense of guilt but who are in fact blameless. We call them 'scrupulous' and they too need to be liberated. They cannot recall a particular sin or something wrong in their lives which was destroying their inner peace, but they have a pervading sense of unworthiness and uncleanness in their own eyes, and therefore much more in God's eyes. Healing from this fear of false guilt is extremely difficult to deal with or to analyse. Jimmy immediately comes to mind as an example of this type of fear. I met him at an El Shaddai service. He was standing at the back of the church, near the door, ready to make his escape when I approached him. His head was stooped and as I started to say a short prayer with him, I noticed how physically cold he was. I asked him gently to lift his head and as he slowly did so, I found myself looking into the saddest eyes I had seen in years. I told him that God loved him in a very special way and that I was privileged to share with him. I asked him if I could lay my hands on him for healing. He said nothing, but his eyes pleaded for me to do so. As I did, I knew that he was miraculously healed of a burden he had been carrying for years.

He was at the healing service the next day and was again at the back of the church. This time he looked and was different. He stood erect, his head held high, and if ever a man was at peace with himself it was Jimmy. He gave me a big smile and I just couldn't believe the change in him. I spoke privately with him afterwards and I asked him how old he was. He told me he was twenty-seven, but the previous day he had looked like someone in his mid fifties. Was his healing a temporary flash in the pan? Eight years afterwards Jimmy is on our healing team when we visit a church in his area. His great gift is his belief that in Jesus we are 'a new creation' (2 Corinthians 5:17). Jimmy is what I call a 'born again' Christian because it was only when he began to believe in himself, and that God loves him as a Father, that he began to live.

We all have a right to ask for and live in Christ's peace. 'Peace I bequeath to you, my own peace I give you, a peace the world cannot give, this is my gift to you.' (John 14:27) It is something very precious which no one should take from us, least of all should we deny it to ourselves. A rigorous church-goer once told me that we were in danger of losing our sense of sin and guilt, whereas I told him we were taking our eyes off our Christian privilege of forgiveness. He shook his head sadly and said he regarded me as a modern heretic. This really brought home to me how far we had strayed from the Christian gospel of the forgiveness of sin by Christ's saving wounds. If we do not forgive ourselves, then we place a barrier between ourselves and God. This barrier of distrust based on false guilt has to be lived and loved away. It is often a slow process. Why is it that we are not encouraged in many churches to love and forgive ourselves? We are constantly being told how sinful we are and in dire need of doing penance, but rarely are we reminded that we must be true to our Christian calling of loving ourselves. Meister Eckhart has got it right: '*If you love yourself, you love everybody else as you do yourself. As long as you love another person more than you love yourself, you will not really succeed in loving yourself, but if you love all alike, including yourself, you will love them as one person and that one person is both God and Man.*' Our love, not only for others and God, but of ourselves, suffers when we are burdened with false guilt by which we diminish ourselves in our own estimation. If we really love God as our forgiving Father, then we cannot allow false guilt to build a barrier between us by not forgiving ourselves. When I forgive myself then the peace which comes to me as a result of my awareness of who I am helps me to bring peace to everyone round me. Peace flows like a river to others when I allow it first of all to flow through me. Jesus came to bring pardon and peace to you and me and it is in him that we find our peace towards each other.

Most people find it extremely difficult to share their pain and shame about the past with others, even their closest friends or members of their family. It is too personal, and they do not want to risk losing the love of the person with whom they share. It is for this reason that in our El Shaddai services we make the sacrament of reconciliation available to those who want privacy and an assurance of the strictest confidence. After all, in the final analysis, guilt is between the individual person's conscience and God. It is, however, a great help to healing if we are able to share our experiences with someone whom we can trust completely and who will show understanding and compassion. People suffocated by false guilt are so self-condemnatory that they are relieved when they are able to talk about it to someone who listens without condemning them. It is a burden shared. When people trust me with their confidence I feel not only healed myself, but am also aware of the responsibility of trying to be like Jesus would be to the person who is burdened by guilt.

From experience, however, I am against sharing inmost and secret thoughts with a group, nor do I favour individuals standing up in front of others to confess what awful people they were before they were converted to the Christian faith. It smacks of exhibitionism and a perverted sense of spiritual arrogance. I am uneasy with those who seem to glory in their past wickedness. It seems to be much more Christian when, in our hearts, we give thanks to the Father who has brought us, like the prodigal son, back home to his house and love. Our gratitude is expressed in the way we live rather than in words. While I agree with the power of testimony, it is as a rule better done privately than trumpeted from a platform. I find it disquieting when people seem to get a kick out of parading themselves in public to witness what God has done for them and their previously sordid way of life. The father received the prodigal son back home without any long explanations to him or anyone else.

The sharing in depth of talking about ourselves and our weaknesses is highly charged emotionally, and I have seen people cry openly as they remember their past and talk about it for the first time. Unfortunately, many married people who come to us for inner healing are unable to share their guilt feelings with their partner. It may concern an affair in the past, or an adopted child from a previous relationship unknown to their partner, or anything else from the past, about which the other partner knows nothing. There still remains the desire to share because they want to be completely open and honest with the person they love. What is the best thing to do in such circumstances? Each case is so unique and personal that it is impossible to give a hard-and-fast rule which applies to every situation. Let me tell you about Joan. It may help you to understand what I mean.

Joan had a very unhappy childhood. Her parents were poor and there was constant quarrelling between them mainly because of the father's uncontrollably violent temper. When she was eighteen, Joan came to England and had a brief relationship with a divorced man in which she conceived a son. Under pressure from people round her, she reluctantly agreed to have the baby adopted. She did not even see him or hold him in her arms. The trauma stayed with her all her life. She never told anyone, especially her family because she knew they just would not understand. In her own words she 'started to live a lie'. She watched with envy mothers happy with their children and she began to feel bitter, especially after she had a hysterectomy. Joan loved children and now she knew she could never have any. In her early thirties, just when she thought that life had passed her by, she met and fell in love with Tim. They were ideally suited and Joan yearned to tell him about her son, but she was afraid he would not understand. Her sense of loss and inability to share with him was so intense that at times she became moody and depressed and was unable to tell him why. In desperation she came to see me and shared her secret. The tears flowed and in them she found a partial healing.

I advised her to bring her husband to a healing service without, as yet, telling him of her past. When I met him and prayed with him I soon realised that he had put Joan on such a pedestal that if she were to tell him her secret it would jeopardise her marriage. Tim, even though a very good man who loved Joan, was just not geared to understanding what had happened in the past. Joan appreciated the situation and now that she has shared her secret with someone, she is able to face life a much freer person in herself. The pain is still there, but she no longer carries it alone. In a very special way she has learned to share her life more deeply with Jesus whom she has come to look on as her friend. She has grown in faith through the experience and her healing is what I call a 'minor miracle'.

There are many Joans in our society who have to keep their secrets to themselves, secrets that bring with them an overpowering sense of shame and guilt far more destructive of their inner peace than that caused by Joan's past. Many women who come to our healing services have been sexually abused by their fathers, brothers, uncles, even grandfathers, and the memory of what happened at a very impressionable period of their lives haunts them. It disturbs their inner peace at its deepest level. They are prisoners who need to be set free, but for whom the image of God as a loving Father is impossible to reconcile with their experience or to believe in because of their past. Their reactions range from a total loathing and blaming of themselves for what happened to them, to despising the person or persons who abused them.

Mary is a typical example of someone whose life was blighted because she was sexually abused by her father from the age of ten. Mary was the eldest of seven children, four of whom were girls. At first she thought her father's approach was one of affection, but this interpretation was soon dispelled by his violent sexual activity. He threatened her with all sorts of punishment if she told anyone, especially her mother, and so she had to remain silent. 'I never knew what it was to grow up,' she told me. 'My father took that away from me.' Mary yearned to tell her mother about what was happening, but there was something about her mother's attitude which kept her from saying anything. Later, to add to her misery, she discovered that her mother knew all the time. When her other sisters in their time were also abused by her father, Mary felt even more guilty because she could say or do nothing about it. She was trapped in a horrible, soul-destroying situation.

When eventually she left home, she soon discovered how damaged her life had become. She was unable to make friends and became more and more withdrawn in herself. She broke off all contact with her family, but still worried about what was happening to her sisters and tormented herself with the guilt of not having the courage to speak out. She never had boyfriends because any sign of affection from boys brought back horrific memories of her lustful father. Eventually she met Bob, whom she married. Mary did not invite any of her family to the wedding and made up an excuse to Bob which he accepted. He knew she was hurt in her home life, but did not want to harass her with questions. They had two lovely children and everything seemed to be going well until Bob noticed that Mary was becoming more withdrawn in herself. He took her to counsellors, but Mary was unable to bring herself to talk about the agony she was suffering inside. A friend suggested that she come to an El Shaddai healing service. Mary took up the story from there.

'Your talk of God as a loving Father, instead of healing me, made me feel more bitter than I already was. How could he be a Father and let those dreadful things happen to my sisters and myself. I never knew a father because I lived with a monster. I wanted to stand up in church and shout you down. You were talking a lot of make-believe and rubbish. How I lasted through the service I shall never know. I vowed never to return to another service, but I did. You spoke the next time about how we are all damaged and are victims living in a hostile world. This made sense to me and I half listened. Then when you came round the church and prayed over me while those who were with you touched me gently, I knew that there was love in the world and that I was unfortunate in my childhood. I know I am being healed of my nightmarish childhood, but I have not forgiven myself yet for my silence and lack of courage about my sisters. I blame myself for what happened to them. I have not told Bob yet but that will come with time. I am still quite bitter about my father, but please, God, that will change. I am beginning to forgive myself, but I do not see God as a father yet. To me he is a friend, but I do talk to him.'

Mary's healing is still going on, but this area is so sensitive that a lot of prayer, gentleness and discernment are needed. Each person, like Mary, who suffered such hurtful memories, has to come to terms within themselves and realise that until they love and forgive themselves and others in a truly human, Christian way, they will never live at peace with themselves. If they are to live in the present, they need to be able to see the past with its hurtful memories as a desert experience from, and through, which they have to learn to grow. Gradually they will realise how necessary it is to forgive themselves or those who have hurt them because forgiveness is of the essence of the healing of hurtful memories. They will need to be patient with themselves because it takes a long time. We will never be healed unless we enter sympathetically as best we can into the mind and heart of the one who damaged us, because the hurtful memories will remain unless we heal them through forgiveness. When we empty ourselves of our anger, hatred, desire for revenge or other bitter feelings which disturb and destroy us inside, then the gentle ointment of God's loving mercy will soothe our injured emotions and spirits. Whenever we pray for the healing of hurtful memories and irrational guilt, we need to begin with a prayer of forgiveness. 'When you stand in prayer, forgive whatever you have against anybody, so that your Father in heaven may forgive your failings too.' (Mark 11:25)

In hurtful *memories* we have to *forgive others*, but above all, we have to *forgive ourselves*. From experience over the years, I have found that forgiving and loving ourselves, even more than forgiving others, is extremely sensitive and fragile, probably more so than any other form of healing ministry. This is why deep prayer for the gift of discernment is essential in such situations. We live in the present and it is difficult to cope with memories of the past which pull us back to those hurtful occasions where we were damaged as persons. When we remember them negatively, we are opening the wound and allowing it to fester. Jesus said that each day has enough troubles of its own, and when we have healed our hurtful memories and false guilt, we must not resurrect them in their hurtful form. If we do not grow from the past by the healing of memories and false guilt, then we condemn ourselves to inflicting on others the damage we ourselves have suffered. The battered child in time becomes the violent parent.

While forgiveness is of the essence of the healing of memories, nevertheless there are other crucial emotional factors involved which need to be dealt with before healing can take place. These are the feelings of anger and guilt which cripple and damage those plagued by hurtful memories. Joan and Mary were justifiably angry with the treatment they had received from their family situation, especially from their parents. They were not given a fair start in life and, even after their sincere forgiveness of those who wronged them, today years afterwards they still bear the scars of what happened in their lives. If I told them at the outset that they had to forgive without allowing them to work through their emotions then, even though they said that they forgave their parents, they would, through no fault of their own, still feel the bitterness in their hearts of what happened to them. Their psychological condition would be worsened and they would sink even deeper into the mire of self-guilt and condemnation. It would be like telling a paraplegic that he could walk if only he had faith.

Forgiveness is a word too easily on the lips of many who minister healing because they fail to acknowledge the area of damage in the person who comes to them for help. We are dealing with a person for whom his past will always be very much part of his life. The healing and forgiveness teach us how to deal with it and to integrate it into our lives, but not to ignore it. If we do then it will surface again in later life in a much more destructive form. Of course, Joan and Mary wanted to be healed of their terrible past, but there was no quick route, no cutting corners. Mary and Joan today realise that though their parents were wrong, there was no point in reliving the past. Slowly they learned to let the past die, even though the scars remained. Before any healing could take place they had to deal with the hurt inside themselves which caused them to feel guilty or ashamed. This was true of Joan because of her relationship with a divorced man and the fact that she allowed her child to be adopted, owing to pressure from others. It was even more so with Mary. She often wondered if she had encouraged her father, but more than that she felt guilty about not speaking up and protecting her younger sisters from the same terrible fate. Both Joan and Mary were able to come through this painful stage, which was not easy for them. They suffered all the painful stresses of withdrawal much as a drug addict or an alcoholic does. I warned them not to touch that memory again because of the consequences which would follow. When these two stages of anger and guilt have been worked through, then the healing power of forgiveness can really take place. They both understood through the healing ministry that what they needed most was inner peace which could only be achieved by forgiving themselves and those who hurt them. This latter forgiveness could not gloss over the past as if it never happened. They both committed their parents to God's mercy and found their own healing by allowing the wounded Christ to show them how they could grow through their hurts and beyond.

Both Mary and Joan have grown like orchids in the desert and today are active in the El Shaddai ministry, helping others in similar circumstances to come out of the darkness into Christ's light of forgiveness and peace. Their first reaction was anger and resentment towards everything and everyone round them. They felt cheated of their parents' love, one of the most precious things in life. They missed out on life and in reality they were as handicapped, if not more so, than a child with some serious physical disability. They were emotionally abused. Because of what happened to them they were unable in later life to share their childhood years with those whom they loved. Others would probably share photographs or stories that warmed their hearts, but for Mary and Joan there was the silence which chilled or the pretence that all had been perfect as they embarked on living a lie which tore them apart inside. The time for talking of forgiveness will arrive only when they realise that living in the past with its hurtful memories is destructive of their peace and happiness. Mary told me, 'I often lay awake at night thinking of what my father did to me and I wished him in hell, while he was probably sleeping at home in his bed. I relived what happened to me so many times that the memory was far worse and more hurtful than the actual physical abuse I suffered at his hands when I was young. My reaction was crippling me and destroying my relationship with Bob and the children. My Christian faith was affected as well because I could not pray to a God who allowed all this to happen to me and yet wanted me to forgive and forget.'

A hurtful memory from the past, like a thorn from a rosebush which pierces our flesh, has to be withdrawn and this is only, and finally, achieved through forgiveness which has love at its source. Christian love of ourselves instils in us our desire for inner peace. It takes the stinging pain out of hurtful memories and false guilt and helps us to forgive ourselves and others. When we are loved in a family by our parents then we will be more secure in ourselves and able to cope more effectively with situations which occur in later life. If we have never known true family love then we are an easy prey for all those things which hurt and diminish us; unlike Jesus in his family life at Nazareth, we will not grow 'in wisdom, in stature and in favour with God and men' (Luke 2:52). If we have experienced forgiveness from our parents when we did things which hurt them, then we find it easy to forgive other people who, whether deliberately or otherwise, have damaged us. We will look on God as our loving, forgiving Father because we have seen his image in our parents for whom Jesus was part of our family. When we allow him to walk with us into the darkness of our past, he will take away our fear caused by false guilt and hurtful memories. He will light up our lives from within, and with him beside us, we will see 'a new heaven and a new earth . . . The world of the past has gone.' (Revelation 21:1,4)

13

Fear of Death

The greatest fear we face is death. It can so control us that we become obsessed by it. As we grow older we become more and more concerned with death rather than with life. We hear of the death of school friends with whom we shared so many happy memories and it brings us up sharply, wondering whether it will be our turn next. Yet there is no age for dying, no time. The only certainty is that it will come. No one has escaped it yet and neither will we. People may have face-lifts to cover up the wrinkles, but deep inside, though they may try to deceive others, the slowing down of their bodily activity and the lapses of memory are something which they cannot escape. A few years ago I telephoned a couple with whom I had been very friendly as a young priest, but somehow or other we had lost touch, apart from Christmas cards. I was giving a mission in their area and thought it would be good to see them again. The wife was her usual happy-go-lucky, friendly self on the phone and when I brought up the idea of calling in to see them she paused and said, 'Michael, we would rather you didn't. Ted has not been well for some time and I'm crippled with arthritis. We would rather you remembered us as we were.' There was pain in her voice. I saw her point. We had 'grown old' and our memories were of the past when we were young and life stretched before us. The wanted to preserve the memory of the happy days of our youth together and when I wrote to them later I told them that for me they would never be old because a friend sees beyond the wrinkles and the slow movements of the body. Since then we have been in touch regularly on the phone, but we did not meet each other face to face so that our memories of happy days when we were in our twenties would remain intact. The phone call set me thinking as to whether or not there was a Christian approach to growing old. I would like to share my thoughts with you.

The Christian life is a series of growing-points, some more special than others, but through all the stages we become more human, more Christian. God is in all those growing-points and Jesus points out the way for us to follow. Jesus said: 'I am the Way; I am Truth and Life. No one can come to the Father except through me.' (John 14:6) Everything in life from beginning to end is *healthy*, even death itself, once I learn to live life to the full one day at a time. The so-called limitations of old age, even death itself, can be used as liberating events setting me free to live because the Christian faith is not about death, but about life.

Why are people outwardly so vain, inwardly so frightened of growing old? As Christians we do not grow old, we just grow in life through our experiences as persons. The body, however important though it be, is only part of who we are. It puzzles me why we are so afraid of growing old. Is it because death cannot be all that far away? Yet death is no respecter of persons or ages. The baby dies at birth, the old person lives through another day, asleep in a chair in an old people's home, and death haphazardly puts its scythe in wherever it chooses, harvesting whoever it meets. To be afraid of death is ultimately destructive of life when it is the dominant theme affecting our minds and emotions. The story is told of a traveller who met the Angel of Death outside a city ravaged by plague and asked him how many had died. 'Forty thousand' came the reply. 'And did they all die of the plague?' asked the traveller. 'No, only ten thousand,' said the

Angel. 'And the other thirty thousand? How did they die?' was the next puzzled question. 'Oh,' said the Angel, 'they died of fear.' If we are afraid of growing old because ultimately we are afraid of death, then surely the best advice is to enjoy life every moment of every day. Joy in living never grows old. You can be old at thirty if your attitude to life is wrong. You can also be young at any age. Life does not begin at forty; it begins at the dawn of each new day. Do not talk about how things were when you were young. It is your world today as well as it was yesterday and will be tomorrow. There are advantages and disadvantages in every age. The day I became a senior citizen I bought a rail card which is as important to me as the card I carried as a student. I don't want to be a day older or a day younger than I am today. Despite all its sham, I still believe in Louis Armstrong's song 'What a wonderful world'. What is important is not the number of years we live but the quality of life. Why have we to die? Why can't we go on living for ever? The simple answer is that, however well we live our lives, we are still 'aliens' and this world is not the perfect place it would have been were there no sin. We die in order to live again where there is no death. This is my Christian belief. Death is another stage in my growing.

My earthly life is a grain of mustard seed which must die in order that I may grow and live a newer, fuller life. When in faith, I see death as a precondition of living, then the fear of death has no control over me. In fact, I am not afraid of it anymore. 'When this perishable nature [our bodies] has put on imperishability, and this mortal nature has put on immortality, then the words of scripture will come true: 'Death is swallowed up in victory. Death, where is your victory? Death, where is your sting?' (1 Corinthians 15:54–55) Unless the seed of my earthly life dies, then all I shall have left is the seed itself which was meant to be put into the soil and die so that it may produce a newer, fuller life. 'Someone may ask, "How are dead people raised, and what sort of body do they have when they come?" How foolish. Whatever you sow must die before it is given new life and what you sow is not the body that is to be but only a bare grain of wheat; it is God who gives it the sort of body that he has chosen for it.' (1 Corinthians 15:35–37). Life has never-ending possibilities for each day and each age.

I don't have to wait until I die before I live the life of the resurrection. It is here now in me, in my world, even though I need my faith to believe in its presence. 'Always, wherever we may be, we carry with us in our body the death of Jesus, so that the life of Jesus, too, may always be seen in our body.' (2 Corinthians 4:10) I don't want to anticipate my death. It will come in God's 'good time', but until that day arrives I shall carry on living my life as best I can. A monk who was sweeping the floor was asked by a stranger what he would do if he were told he had a few minutes to live. He replied quite simply, 'I would just carry on sweeping the floor.' Any time is a good time for dying when you know how to live. This is why Christians should always talk of life. Even when death comes into our thoughts we think of it only in terms of life. Those who constantly preach about death have wandered far from the life-giving gospel of Jesus who said: 'I am the resurrection . . . Whoever lives and believes in me will never die.' (John 11: 25–26) Jesus came that we might have life and have it to the full. We were meant, as Christians, to be full of the juice and joy of living. Physical death, when it comes to disturb our earthly existence, is just the final movement to enable us to live life as fully as possible, as God wants us to do. It is the flowering of our true selves which will never wither, the dawn of a new day which will never end. The hymn my father chose for his requiem Mass, appropriate to his life-style, was 'Morning has broken'. How right he was, he had lived through ninety-two winters and summers. Life had not always been easy for him, but he never grew old. He was always young at heart because through his Christian faith, he knew how to live. When death finally disturbed him, he began to live in a peace which nothing would ever disturb again.

Death is the ultimate liberator from all fear because it frees me from the great fear of death itself. In the third century Tertullian said of death, 'there is nothing dreadful in that which delivers us from all that is to be dreaded'. As a Christian who believes in the resurrection, the only way to face death is to live life to the full, not the other way round. I was constantly told in my young, impressionable days that if I wanted to live my life as I should, then I had to keep the thought of my death constantly before my mind. No wonder so many people are depressed and oppressed, and look on God as a threat and a kill-joy. In life the great healing force of the resurrection, so sadly neglected in many aspects of church life, is that it teaches us how to live. Without it there is no healing and death is the ultimate, unavoidable threat. For those who do not believe in life after death, then any 'healing' they receive is only temporary until death comes to eliminate them. In El Shaddai we *celebrate death* as the ultimate healing which prepares us for life without end. Where there is a false teaching on the relationship of life and death we have first of all to help people understand what the Christian life is all about and what the resurrection of Jesus really means. Healing is more difficult in proportion to the extent that the fear of death controls a person's attitude to the way he lives.

Why is it that so many good church-going people have a pagan attitude to death which fills them with an obsessive, controlling fear? We say we believe in the resurrection, but it does not seem to flow into our everyday thinking and daily life. Death, the more we concentrate on it, has a subduing influence on people, filling them with fear, so why do we talk about it so much? For the true Christian, death, like birth, is a cause for celebration. The pain of dying is like that of childbirth: 'A woman in childbirth suffers, because her time has come; but when she has given birth to the child she forgets the suffering in her joy that a man has been born into the world.' (John 16:21)

I think of the many wonderful people whom I have met in our healing services who have gone to their reward with bravery, joy and peace. I remember Marie, who told me a few days before she died, 'You have helped me to know how to live so that for the last year I have really lived. I have not prepared for death, but when it comes I shall meet it as another blessing from God my Father who gave me life and will never take it away from me!' Marie lived her death as though it was a door leading to another life. This is the best and only Christian way to approach it. The pain which may precede death, like the pangs of childbirth, is more to be feared than death itself. I think that we exaggerate the pain of dying into far more than it really is. When our final time to go home to our Father comes, he will smooth the way for us. I have known the peace of spirit with which truly Christian people are blessed when they are dying. John told me when he was dying how clearly he saw everything in his life. 'I think I know now why things happened the way they did,' he said. 'You were right, Father, God loves us. I didn't always see it that way but I do now.' John, in his dying, had grown spiritually far more than I had. He was on another plateau where God was closer to him in reality than any words of mine could be. He could see the lights of home and they were reflected in the glow of his face. I have been privileged to be with many Johns on this very special occasion and their going home was a very special healing for me.

People are afraid of death because we doubt whether there is anything beyond the grave. If there is no life after death then what is there to hope for? A people without hope is, of course, doomed to fear. The whole of the teaching of the Early Church is that our Christian hope is based on the resurrection of Jesus Christ. St Paul emphasised time and again that 'the mystery is Christ among you, your hope of glory' (Colossians 1:27). 'Take a firm grip on the hope that is held out to us. Here we have an anchor for our soul, as sure as it is firm, and reaching right through beyond the veil where Jesus has entered before us and on our behalf' (Hebrews 6:18–20). We are people who live and die in hope, a hope that is based on the life, death and resurrection of Jesus Christ. If we fear death then how can we say we are a people of Christian hope?

I have looked at life after death from many angles. Unless I believe it myself then how can I talk about it with conviction to others, or engage in any meaningful way in the ministry of healing. I have been faced by many hundreds of people who doubt the resurrection, and I have to enter into all the pain of their doubting and allow it to flow into me so that in turn my belief and hope may flow back into them. I have really doubted and been disturbed in the process. Eventually my faith in life after death has strengthened and so has my hope which is for me a liberating force for real joy in living. People quite wrongly have guilt feelings concerning their doubts about life after death, whereas I believe that the very questioning itself helps us to a deeper penetration of the great mystery of our faith in the resurrection of Jesus, on which our life in this world and the next hinges. Even the apostles themselves doubted the resurrection of Jesus from the dead: 'Lastly, he showed himself to the Eleven themselves while they were at table. He reproached them for their incredulity and obstinacy, because they had refused to believe those who had seen him after he had risen' (Mark 16:14). For the apostles death was so final that when Jesus died they felt that this was the end of everything. Their complete surrender to the absoluteness of death is a crumb of comfort for us in our doubting. Their doubt seems to excuse our own. The most obvious case of doubt concerns Thomas, who has since been given the prefix 'Doubting' (John 20:24–29). I like to call him 'believing' Thomas. St Gregory, commenting on the slow surrender of Thomas, sees it as a 'great help to strengthening our faith because his act of faith is fuller and more explicit than any other confession of faith in the resurrection recorded in the Gospels'. The unwillingness too of the apostles to believe the reports of the empty tomb is only overcome when the risen Jesus stands in their midst.

Each one of us has to set the strength of our faith in the risen Lord against the finality of physical death in order to determine which is stronger. It is the final encounter between faith and fear. Even when I believe in life after death some fear of death may still remain, but at least I shall know it for what it is. My faith in everlasting life will increase, and my fear of death decrease as my personal belief in the resurrection of Jesus grows. If I am an Easter person, and really believe in life everlasting, then I should thrill with joy since I would have conquered the fear of the ultimate, which is death. The world, in the face of such faith, would begin to hope again in the true value of life as we Christians live it. As it is we Christians are often a hunched-up congregation overburdened with sin and guilt who come to church every week in order to 'hedge our bets'. Religion does not make us happy because it enslaves rather than liberates us.

Even though we believe in life after death the nagging doubt still remains. This doubt or fear has to be brought out into the open and challenged by faith. Those who doubt challenge my faith, and if few share their doubts with me then perhaps it is a clear indication that maybe they think that I too have little faith in life everlasting and they are afraid to talk to me lest the rock on which they built their faith is only made of shifting sand. Life after death is the most wonderful promise held out to Christians, and yet we share our hopes with so relatively few. It is quite surprising how many good church-going people have reservations about life after death. Recently I met a missioner's wife who quite categorically stated that her dead husband 'was no more'. She believed that 'he had his heaven on earth and when he died that was the end of him'. She was devoid of Christian hope, and was no better than the Sadducees who did not believe in life after death. St Paul reminded the Sanhedrin at his trial in Jerusalem: 'It is for our hope in the resurrection of the dead that I am on trial' (Acts 23:6).

Even though we may think that we firmly believe in life after death our peace of soul may be disturbed by the death of a loved one. This is quite a common phenomenon which, when the time comes, we will learn to grow through. A typical case which illustrates this point concerns an excellent Christian whose husband died tragically after nearly twenty years of very happily married life. She seemed lost for a long time afterwards, and no longer seemed to be alive because she had lost her peace of soul. The friends who were constant callers after his death no longer came to visit her as frequently as before, and she was left more or less to face her sorrows alone. She continued her church work with more vigour rather than less, probably in order to help her to forget herself and her sorrow. She began to draw in on herself, and felt her home was a prison with memories of her husband. Yet she was afraid to go out socially because everything was a painful reminder of him. One day we were talking about life after death, and while she blindly professed her belief in the resurrection, I kept on asking her why she was so sure, and if so why was she so sad? Eventually she broke down and confessed that she wondered herself if her husband was still alive. We read and prayed together – I Corinthians, chapter 15 – and her tears which flowed were of joy rather than sorrow. 'Now,' she said, 'I believe that Jack is alive and we will never be parted.' She was a different person from that day onwards, when she truly believed that for her husband, as for all who die in Christ, *life is changed, not taken away.*

As I grow older I am not so much afraid of death as the manner of my dying, because basically I am afraid of suffering. I was told as a young man studying for the priesthood to picture myself in my last agony, far away from my friends and loved ones, an image that chilled my heart and disturbed my inner peace. I do not agree with this approach to spirituality which breeds fear, and the relics of it are still deeply ingrained in me and in many Catholic priests. It does not take into account that when my turn comes to die the Lord will be with me as I pass through the valley of darkness. What really disturbed my peace in my youth, however, was the death of my mother. Her death cast its shadow over the whole family a long time before it happened. At the impressionable age of fourteen, through wearying weeks and months, I watched her disintegrate physically and finally die. I hated to see her suffer, and yet I was aware that I was power-less to help her. For months I dreaded the tension which eventually would come when the moment of death arrived. The picture of it is still vivid in my memory, as indeed is the peace with which she left our world. I bless my father that he told me what was happening to her, and took me step by step along the way.

As a priest I have suffered with and for dying people because those closest to them refused to share with them the truth of their physical condition when it was kinder and necessary for them to do so. Everyone then pro-ceeded to live a sham, so that an artificial atmosphere was created which is a positive harm to everyone, especially the dying. If only we were more sensitive to each other, then we would know what is required of us, and so share the last precious days with our loved ones at a depth that would enrich us all.

I had to tell my father and eldest sister, Mary, that they were dying, and I am convinced from my experience that they were helped by my honesty and support and that, therefore, it was right for me to do so. We talked about death in a creative way so that they were helped to die more easily. Our relationship was unique through the sharing not only of pain, but of our deep faith in the resurrection. Through the Christian manner of their dying they diminished my own fear of it. I certainly want to be told when I am dying since I believe it is my right, as well as a gift, which helps me to prepare for my meeting with my Father, in whom I shall find my fullness of peace.

Death will always remain, of course, a test of faith of the *bereaved*, and for a time I found it hard to accept the deaths of my parents and sister at the particular time. Mourning does not bring back the dead to life on earth, and so in common with everyone else I had to learn to live with my loss, knowing that my grief would mellow as I picked up the pieces of my life again, and moved forward in my daily living.

It is wrong, as some Christian ministers have done, *to minimise bereavement.* The way I have heard some of them preach unfeelingly at funerals has made me wonder whether they have ever experienced the panic, the emotional tension, the periods of depression, the stark moments when death seems to haunt us with its apparent triumph because death for a time is uppermost in the lives of the bereaved. It is in such moments that, heartbreaking though it may be, people must go on believing in life after death, when every natural inclination opposes it, and when only the bereaved themselves know a pain in their hearts which can be experienced and not described. They may even be told to snap out of it, but wounds of the heart take a long time to heal before a new peace in a new situation can be found.

There is no panacea for bereavement since each one is unique, with its own peculiar set of circumstances. Eventually our lives will settle back to a more even keel, and the life and death of our loved one will take on more realistic proportions. It is how we lived with them in life that will determine our attitude to them in death. It is not wrong to mourn the death of our loved ones, but St Paul reminds us: 'Make sure you do not grieve about them, like the other people who have no hope' (1 Thessalonians 4:13). Weeping over the death of a loved one is not against our faith in the resurrection. At the death of Lazarus Jesus wept, and the Jews said, 'See how much he loved him' (John 11:36). Tears are necessary to afford the bereaved a relief from tension, but tears should not overshadow the belief in the resurrection which is there as an anchor when they are cast about on a sea of emotions.

There are two choices for the bereaved: to live in grief and remorse, with an uncontrollable sense of guilt that they had not been as kind to the deceased as they should have been, or to face their feelings and work them through. Jesus, after he had wept, took over the leadership in order to help the bereaved Mary and Martha: 'Take the stone away' (John 11:39). We have to get on with living despite our awareness that in the death of our loved one we have lost part of ourselves. In a sense it is true that we have to 'leave the dead to bury their dead' (Matthew 8:22). This may sound cruel, but we cannot spend the rest of our lives in unproductive remorse; our loved ones would not have it that way.

The churches could do much more in assisting the bereaved to recover their peace of mind, and to use the occasion to help them deepen their faith in life after death. If churches placed Jesus more at the centre of their preaching, then his resurrection would be the focus of attention in our thoughts and prayers, rather than our own death. Perhaps as Roman Catholics we placed too great an emphasis on the importance of Christmas, and looked on Easter more as the end of Lent rather than the celebration of our own *personal* victory over death in the person of Jesus Christ. The reformed liturgy is helping to redress the balance, but we have a long way to go before our people will become filled with the power of their resurrection in Christ the Lord. For many years the person of Jesus holding back the stone of the tomb letting in the light of his Father's love to dispel the darkness of death, is the picture I have kept before me in my journey through life. When I am buried in my tomb by men, then with the risen Jesus I pass through the open door on the other side to my heavenly home. *Jesus is my resurrection*. As a Christian I believe, like the Jews, in life after death, but more than that I believe that my resurrection comes through the person of Jesus Christ because, like peace, it is his precious gift to me as his follower. He says to me, 'I am the resurrection', and the life I share with him is in his risen body.

The church that does not highlight sufficiently the central role of Christ in our *personal resurrection* must obviously condemn its followers to an obsessive interest in, and fear of, death. The more we preach death, the less we preach life. How few sermons have we heard about heaven for which we are destined, while hell, which is not our home, is preached far too often? The preacher sometimes merely projects his own personal fears, and many people have got hang-ups on death, judgement and hell which not only seriously interfere with their spiritual lives but also cripple their attitude to life itself and destroy their peace of soul. They cannot live their lives to the full because of the fear that it will soon end and afterwards – nothing.

The message of St Paul and the Early Church is simple and triumphant: Jesus in his person has given every Christian new life through his death and resurrection. When I live in the light of this liberating truth then I shall grow in the personal love of Jesus throughout my life. I shall be so close to him when death comes that I shall see it as a dissolving in order to be with him fully and for ever. The only thing that will be disturbed will be the tent of my mortal body. Death will have been swallowed up in victory. Peace will reign for ever.

14

Jesus Heals Fear Through Us

Jesus heals today. He is faithful to his promises. He is with us always. His essential teaching will always remain the same. Jesus is a healer. He calls his followers to be ministers of his healing. Just as Jesus heals the person, so do we as Christians. If we fail to do this then our lives would not mirror his. During his life on earth Jesus used healing as the most powerful means to proclaim his gospel. He knows we need it too if people are to believe in God as a loving Father. That is why he gave his apostles power to heal when he sent them out to preach his gospel. 'He called the twelve together and gave them power and authority over all devils and to cure diseases, and he sent them out to proclaim the Kingdom and to heal' (Luke 9:1–2). In other words we are not really proclaiming the Kingdom if we do not believe in, or practise, Christ's mission of healing. Jesus was generous with his gift of healing. He did not confine it to the apostles. He gave it also to the seventy-two disciples when they set out in pairs to proclaim the Kingdom. 'Cure those who are sick, and say, "The Kingdom of God is very near to you".' (Luke 10:9–10). People experience the presence of God in healing.

Our ministry of healing is authenticated because its authority comes from Jesus himself. Knowing that his healing demonstrated in a unique way God's love for us, Jesus wanted this healing to go on to the end of time among his followers who believed in him and his abiding power and presence. By this healing power people would know that the risen Christ was present among his followers. In his name the Early Church was born and grew. St Peter healed the beggar who was crippled from birth with these words, ' "I have neither silver nor gold, but I will give you what I have: in the name of Jesus Christ the Nazarene, walk!" Instantly his feet and ankles became firm, he jumped up, stood, and began to walk, and he went with them into the Temple, walking and jumping and praising God' (Acts 3:6–8). Why do some people try to limit the healing power of Christ to his lifetime, or that of the Early Church? There is nothing in the gospel about this temporary phase in the mission of Christ and his followers. On the contrary it was expected that it would increase and intensify in future ages as those who believed would obey Christ's command, 'Go out to the whole world; proclaim the Good News to all creation ... These are the signs that will be associated with believers; ... they will lay their hands on the sick, who will recover' (Mark 16:16–18). I am certain that if we had the faith necessary for the ministry of healing then many more people would be healed, and would experience the Good News for themselves. They would know that the risen Jesus was alive today in our Church and world. If we really believe in the promises of Jesus then there is no escaping the consequences of his promise to continue healing in his Church through his followers.

> You must believe me when I say
> that I am in the Father and the Father is
>   in me;
> believe it on the evidence of this work, if
>   for no other reason.
> I tell you most solemnly,
> whoever believes in me
> will perform the same works as I do myself,
> he will perform even greater works,

because I am going to the Father,
Whatever you ask for in my name I will do,
so that the Father may be glorified in the Son.
If you ask for anything in my name,
I will do it.

(John 14:11–14)

If this promise is not fulfilled today in us and our
Church then we have no gospel to preach. Jesus would
become the purveyor of empty promises and we would go
on asking in his name and never receive an answer. But
if his promise is true, then whenever or wherever two or
three meet in his name then he will be there with them
(Matthew 18:20.)

However, if we do not believe this promise of Jesus then
we will not ask, or our faith may be so limited that even
though we believe that Jesus is among us, nevertheless,
apart from the sacraments he is not healing his people
because we believe that healing ended centuries ago in
the Early Church. If we believe that he is with his followers
always when they are forgiving sins in his name then
through them he is also healing his people just as he did
during his own lifetime. Both promises are equally valid
and *permanent* signs of Christ's followers. There is no men-
tion in any of the gospels that all forms of healing exercised by Christ's immediate followers were less necessary
today and would end after a certain period of time. Healing of the person in order to make him whole and the
forgiving of sins were essentially connected. They were to
be seen as distinguishing marks of Christ's community. If
anything, the healing of people's bodies was the more
predominant not only during Jesus' own lifetime and that
of the apostles, but also of the Early Church. Sadly,
though, a change took place and the Church has tended
to focus more on forgiveness of sins than other forms of
healing.

We must not expect support from institutions which

have neglected, opposed or just do not understand the true nature of Christian healing. It is not their personal fault, but rather the result of teaching and emphasis in the past. This requires, on our part, patience, gentleness and deep trust that God, in his own mysterious way, is healing his people.

> The Lord Yahweh says this: I am going to look after my flock myself and keep all of it in view. As a shepherd keeps all his flock in view when he stands up in the middle of his scattered sheep, so shall I keep my sheep in view. I shall rescue them from wherever they have been scattered during the mist and darkness . . . I shall feed them in good pasturage; the high mountains of Israel will be their grazing ground. I myself will pasture my sheep, I myself will show them where to rest – it is the Lord Yahweh who speaks. I shall be a true shepherd to them. (Ezekiel 34:11–12, 14–16)

The necessary preparation

Because the ministry of all forms of healing, like that of forgiving sins in Christ's name, is of such vital importance in the Church we have to prepare ourselves for this very powerful dynamic ministry in a very special way. The devil, as we know, is only too keen to infiltrate this mission of Christ. Jesus warns us, 'Remember, I am sending you out like sheep among wolves; so be cunning as serpents and yet as harmless as doves' (Matthew 10:16). In our El Shaddai ministry we have met many people, some of them well-intentioned, who have pushed themselves forward as ministers of healing. I believe that the preparation for the ministry of healing takes a long time, just as Jesus himself spent thirty hidden years before he began his public life. He could not have spent his time better. By his example he reminds us that we have to be prepared to wait and to listen for God's gentle call. When the time is right we will hear and answer him. I am suspicious of those who claim to have a gift of healing because of burning sensations in their hands or because they feel the pain in their body for someone whom they claim needs healing. Such signs are authenticated only when seen in the context of the whole life-style of preparation. The qualities required for healing God's people are much deeper than external visible signs. They penetrate the deepest hidden parts of our being, as in the case of Mary the Mother of Jesus, 'a sword will pierce your own soul so that the secret thoughts of many may be laid bare' (Luke 2:35). Those who have suffered in silence know how to listen compassionately to others who stand before them in need of healing. It is a meeting of persons, a soul-to-soul encounter. While we are *all* called as Christians to *pray* for healing for ourselves and for others, and the prayer of the community is intrinsically bound up with healing, nevertheless other forms of the ministry, because they take us into special needs of people, require special preparation in time and testing of our faith. 'Let us not lose sight of Jesus . . . he endured the cross, disregarding the shamefulness of it . . . Think of the way he stood such opposition from sinners and then you will not give up for want of courage . . . Suffering is part of your training; God is treating you as his *sons*. Has there ever been any son whose father did not *train* him?' (Hebrews 12:2–4, 7)

Preparation for the ministry of healing is not a purely cerebral, physical or emotional exercise. It concerns the whole person and it is only in God's special school that we are trained. The best we can do is to co-operate. No one can legislate for, or organise in detail, the ministry of healing. We need *discernment* within ourselves and from others immersed in the ministry so that we may know where the Lord is leading us. Through this God-given gift we hope that we are able to make the right judgement as to those who are ready to share in the El Shaddai ministry. While we are sensitive not to turn anyone away, we give the Lord the benefit of the doubt! We are in constant

need of prayer because we know that our ministry will be
diminished once the wrong people become involved. I
would like to outline for you some of the qualities we
look for in those who wish to share in the ministry of
healing. Since all Christian healing is based on *prayer* I
devoted a whole chapter earlier in the book to this and
its place in the life of everyone involved in the ministry
of healing.

In our minds we must be the same as Christ Jesus
(Philippians 2:5). *Jesus alone is the healer.* We are only his
ministers, the postmen delivering the mail. Once we start
to claim healing in our name and power then we have
put ourselves outside the boundaries of Christ's ministry.
I have met people who claim divine power within themselves who are easy prey for the devil. St Peter, after his
ministry of healing to the crippled beggar, addressed the
people: 'Why are you so surprised at this? Why are you
staring at us as though we had made this man walk by
our own power or holiness? It is in the name of Jesus
which, through our faith in it, has brought back the
strength of this man whom you see here and who is well
known to you. It is faith in that name that has restored
this man to health, as you can all see.' (Acts 3:12–16)
Ministers of healing are ordinary people. They are not to be
regarded by us because of the ministry they exercise as
extraordinary people. Jesus alone is extraordinary. We are
ordinary.

God-centredness

Like Jesus, in healing, we are asked to be God-centred,
to empty ourselves of pride, self-seeking and anything by
which we would intrude ourselves into the healing situation. It is Christ who heals. We are not healers in our
own name and power but in his.

People who mistakenly call themselves 'healers' tend to
stand on higher ground than those to whom they minister.
The holier-than-thou attitude destroys the individual's or

group's ministry of healing. They would never dream of asking a healing ministry from others. Healing for them, either consciously or not, is power. This power-seeking and self-glorification is the most insidious force which seeps through the whole fabric of the healing movement. Healing is an ideal platform from which to launch an ego trip. I know many who lead a Walter Mitty type of exist-ence, whose exaggerated claims are received with such credibility that they even begin to believe them them-selves. People in extreme need of healing are easy targets for such unscrupulous and unchristian behaviour. Anyone who takes on the role-play of a Christian healer in order to carve out a niche for himself is only a *hired man* and 'since he is not the shepherd and the sheep do not belong to him, abandons the sheep and runs away as soon as he sees a wolf coming, and then the wolf attacks and scatters the sheep; this is because he is only a hired man and has no concern for the sheep.' (John 10:12–13)

Jesus, on the other hand, forgot about himself and was humble even to the point of accepting death on a cross. Only then does his Father raise him high. One of the tests of genuineness for us, as an El Shaddai team, is to sit occasionally in the body of the church and receive rather than minister healing. We are all equal in Christ's Church (family) because we are all wounded. If 'God did not spare his own Son, but gave him up to benefit us all' (Romans 8:32), then he will not spare us. Unless and until we suffer in the cause of Christ's ministry then we will never be truly God-centred or appreciate the deep and often hidden value of being a Christian. 'All I want is to know Christ and the power of his resurrection and to share his sufferings by reproducing the pattern of his death.' (Philippians 3:10)

Courage
When Jesus worked his miracles many people from his own village of Nazareth said of him, ' "Where did the

man get this wisdom and these miraculous powers? This is the carpenter's son, surely? Is not his mother the woman called Mary? So where did the man get it all?" And they would not accept him. But Jesus said to them, "A prophet is only despised in his own country and in his own house", and he did not work many miracles there because of their lack of faith.' (Matthew 13:54–58) We have to be discerning enough in the ministry of healing to expect rejection and criticism from those from whom we have a right to expect a Christian response. Many who feel called to the healing ministry soon fall by the wayside because they lack the courage to persevere, or the discernment to know when to pass on to new territory. *We have to stand up and be counted for our belief.* We need to balance the strength of our belief in the ministry of healing against the negative response of people. Our faith will conquer our fear. Christ alone is our hope. His judgement of us is much more important than that of any individual or group. The desire to please others is a very damaging influence obstructing the ministry of healing. We need the courage which comes from faith in the living Lord to find our fulfilment in continuing his ministry in our life and world.

Openness

In his healing Jesus was always open to his Father's will and to the needs of those around him. His words in the garden when he knelt down and prayed, 'Father,' he said 'if you are willing, take this cup away from me. Nevertheless, let your will be done, not mine' (Luke 22:42), show how open he was to whatever demands his Father made of him. Lazarus was his best friend, and yet he left it to his Father to decide whether or not he would raise Lazarus from the dead. Even then it was only 'for the sake of all those who stand round me, so that they may believe it was you who sent me' (John 11:42).

We cannot decide who is to be healed and when. This

is God the Father's province into which we should not be
foolish enough to enter. *We are not to play God.* Probably
because of lack of faith, or an emotional need within
themselves, some ministers of healing make unfounded
claims of physical healing or discernment which damage
the cause of Christ and his healing mission. I know of
several people who claimed to be 'Christian healers' who
have given up their 'belief' in God because the person
for whom they were praying did not physically recover or
died. *They acted God.* In other cases people have been
deluded into thinking they were physically healed and
were advised, even ordered, by the 'healer' to abandon
their medical or other artificial aids which helped to
relieve their pain and distress. Genuine ministers of
Christian healing wait on the Lord, and their ministry is
the result of deep prayer and commitment in faith to
God the Father who is healing his people. When we are
open to him, God works through us. If we are open to
God then he will show us through the gift of discernment
what to say, when, and to whom. God will never be out-
done in generosity. Since God the Father gave us his only
Son then 'we can be certain after such a gift, that he will
not refuse anything he can give.' (Romans 8:32)

God heals his children in a way which we will never
fully understand by a process of reason, but still believe
and accept because of our faith.

Listening

Jesus had an open line twenty-four hours a day with his
Father. 'In the morning, long before dawn, he got up and
left the house, and went off to a lonely place and prayed
there.' (Mark 1:35) Every exercise of inner healing must
be *saturated in prayer* and an awareness that it is God's
children with whom we are dealing. We need to listen to
people as Jesus did rather than rush in with our own
prayer which flows from the surface of self rather than
the depth of God. We listen with our hearts and with *both*

eyes on God. Only then can we look at those to whom we minister. Time and again Jesus asked those who came to him for healing, 'What do you want me to do for you? (Mark 10:51). He knew what they *needed* but he was ready to listen to what they thought they *wanted*. They came for the curing of their bodies and Jesus, seeing them as persons, healed their souls as well (Mark 2:1–12).

It is much more important to listen than to speak. This is why healing services should be filled with the silence of deep prayer, rather than the babble of people in the market place. When we concentrate on God and his unique love for the person before us in need of help, and when we look at them, we are privileged to be there, knowing that it is the Christ in them we see because we have already been blessed and healed to discover him within ourselves. People want to know that we care. It is what they see in us that matters and not so much what we say. Jesus spoke little to those whom he healed. A rush of words from ministers of healing is disturbing and unnecessary. I am always chary of letting anyone pray over me who is not led to do so by deep reflection and prayer.

Sharing

Just as Jesus shared his life, so we too share our lives with him by being prepared to share our lives with others. The ministry of healing is a sharing through identification with Christ and his people. In Christ we share the pain of those who come to us for help. We are all lepers who need Christ's cleansing healing. We cannot pray with someone until we have put ourselves into their situation. Anyone who does not feel the pain of those around him is hardly likely to be called to the ministry of healing. In the ministry of healing we are *compassionate* with those who suffer. Compassion is essential to those in the ministry. They should concentrate on the pain of those to whom God sends them rather than their own problems.

Many delude themselves into thinking that they have a special ministry of healing to those who have suffered a similar situation, whereas in fact, subconsciously, they are using them as pawns for their own parched emotions. It is a freakish form of manipulation and a case of the blind leading the blind. Only those people who have *overcome* their problems and have integrated them into their Christian lives should be encouraged to volunteer for the healing ministry. God will use them in a special way. Because they have travelled in the valley of darkness and have experienced what it is to walk in the light, they are a vital part of Christ's healing ministry. They are a sign of hope and healing to others. The best minister of healing to others is the one so in love with Christ that he sees and loves him in the wounded person who stands before him.

Healing is a sharing of all that we are with all that the wounded are. Jesus shared his joys and sorrows not only with his friends Peter, James and John on the mountain of the Transfiguration (Mark 9:2), and in the Garden of Gethsemane (Mark 14:33), but also with strangers on the cross (Luke 23:39–43). A minister of healing is a sharer. He knows that the one who seeks healing is a wounded Christ, a member of the Christian family. By sharing first with the wounded Lord he can then share more fully with those who are wounded around him.

Believing
We believe that nothing is impossible to God the Father because he knows the needs of those to whom we minister. They may know their *wants* but God will meet their *needs*. Too often we pray for healing for obvious physical or emotional problems in others, while what they really need is deep inner peace which only God can give. Time and again, we know from our experience the importance of discernment. If we put limits on God's healing power then we are in fact barring him from areas which are

rightly his. By listening to him, and the people to whom
we minister, we will know what to pray for, believing that
what we ask will be granted. We should not 'hedge our
bets' but pray directly and with confidence to our Father
who knows what is in our hearts before the words are on
our lips. St James reminds us of the power to heal of
prayers said in faith. 'The prayer of faith will save the sick
man and the Lord will raise him up again; and if he has
committed any sins, he will be forgiven.' (James 5:15)
Our faith will help to rekindle the faith of those to whom
we minister just as they in turn will do the same for us. We
must never in faith ask God for less than he is prepared to
give. The well of healing is limitless.

Love

The love of God the Father for us is the source of all
healing. 'Think of the love that the Father has lavished
on us, by letting us be called God's children; and that is
what we are.' (1 John 3:1) If we are his children then
God wants us whole and healthy as persons. None of
us can love ourselves or anyone else as generously and
completely as God our Father. For this reason we must
be sensitive to the danger of using the healing ministry
to satisfy our own emotional needs. Purely human love
and affection which we feel for others must be shot
through with the healing brightness and warmth of God's
love for his wounded people. God's love for us is uncon-
ditional. It is not a love we merit because of something
good in us. It is his love that flows out from him so that
we might become whole and good. God loves us before we
even attempt to love ourselves or anyone else. It is all his
action to us, not our reaction to him. Healing in our
ministry flows through us because God wants us to be his
channels of grace and peace. We cannot stop him loving
us even though we refuse to love him in return. This is
the mystery of divine love which all ministers of healing
have to understand. If we really experienced God's love

then discernment, courage, and all the other qualities
necessary in a minister of healing would follow. All
followers of Jesus are to be known by this special love
emanating from God the Father through Christ to us,
and through us to others.

> As the Father has loved me,
> so I have loved you.
> Remain in my love.
> This is my commandment:
> love one another,
> as I have loved you.
>
> (John 15:9, 12)

The commandment of Jesus is for us to love each other
as a reflection of God the Father's love for us. Because
we are damaged, unlike Jesus, the best we can do is to
allow this love to flow through us without limiting or
diluting it.

The basis of our El Shaddai ministry is our unshakeable
belief that God is our Father who loves us every moment
of every day in every situation. He knows who and what
we are. He takes us as we are because we can come to
him no other way. *He always heals us.* He brings us the
inner peace of Jesus his Son. Inner peace conquers fear
because it comes from love: not our love of God but his
love for us. Love and fear cannot exist together. They are
incompatible. If we want peace of mind and heart then
all we have to do is to allow God's love to flow into us. It
is a stream of living water which brings us hope, joy and
a new vision of who we are and what life is all about. We
think positively by removing the blockage which fear
causes in our lives. Knowing that God loves us, we call on
him to help us carry our burdens. He will answer. Jesus
said, 'Come to me, all you who labour and are overburdened, and I will give you rest. Shoulder my yoke and
learn from me, for I am gentle and humble in heart,

and you will find rest for your souls. Yes, my yoke is easy and my burden light.' (Matthew 11: 28–30.) Simon of Cyrene helped Jesus to carry his cross. No one carries his cross alone. A burden shared is a burden lightened. When Christ is with us then we have nothing to fear. All is well, and all will be well.

Trust

We trust the final outcome of our healing ministry to God the Father's loving judgement. He knows what is best for each one of us. Just as we are not masters of our own destiny, so also we are not in control of the outcome of any individual healing ministration. In short, God knows best. This was the attitude of Jesus himself. It should be ours also. 'Do not let your hearts be troubled. Trust in God still, and trust in me.' (John 14:1) We do not know what is really good for ourselves or another person because we judge only by appearances.

> 'What father among you would hand his son a stone when he asked for bread? Or hand him a snake instead of a fish? Or hand him a scorpion if he asked for an egg? If you then, who are evil, know how to give your children what is good, how much more will our heavenly Father give the Holy Spirit to those who ask him!' (Luke 11:11–13)

We live in hope that all will be well. If we could only see in faith and love, God the Father is healing us all in a way which surpasses all our dreams and more than supplies our deepest needs. This hope keeps us joyful because all healing is a celebration of Christ's triumph over sin, death and fear.

Further Material on Healing

Books on Healing by Monsignor Michael Buckley

His Healing Touch   (Fount)
Christian Healing   (Catholic Truth Society)
Stories That Heal   (Darton, Longman and Todd)
More Stories That Heal   (Darton, Longman and Todd)
Treasury of the Holy Spirit (Hodder and Stoughton)
Let Peace Disturb You   (St Paul Publications)

Tapes

1. *Healing the Person and God Our Healing Father*
2. *Healing and Suffering and the Healing Community*
3. *Healing in the Parish* (Canon Jimmy Collins)
   The El Shaddai Ministry (Oonagh Watters)
4. *The Peace of Christ and I Believe in Healing*
5. *The Healing of Fear and the Healing of False Guilt*
6. *Healing is Loving Yourself*
7. *Praying for Healing*
8. *Healing Brings Hope and Joy*
   Trusting God

All tapes except Tape 3 are by Monsignor Michael Buckley

For further information contact:
    'El Shaddai'
    9 West Ridings
    East Preston
    West Sussex BN16 2TD